Marc Sniukas

Reshaping Strategy

Marc Sniukas

Reshaping Strategy

Exploring the Content, Process and Context of Strategic Innovation

VDM Verlag Dr. Müller

Impressum/Imprint (nur für Deutschland/ only for Germany)
Bibliografische Information der Deutschen Nationalbibliothek: Die Deutsche Nationalbibliothek verzeichnet diese Publikation in der Deutschen Nationalbibliografie; detaillierte bibliografische Daten sind im Internet über http://dnb.d-nb.de abrufbar.

Alle in diesem Buch genannten Marken und Produktnamen unterliegen warenzeichen-, marken- oder patentrechtlichem Schutz bzw. sind Warenzeichen oder eingetragene Warenzeichen der jeweiligen Inhaber. Die Wiedergabe von Marken, Produktnamen, Gebrauchsnamen, Handelsnamen, Warenbezeichnungen u.s.w. in diesem Werk berechtigt auch ohne besondere Kennzeichnung nicht zu der Annahme, dass solche Namen im Sinne der Warenzeichen- und Markenschutzgesetzgebung als frei zu betrachten wären und daher von jedermann benutzt werden dürften.

Coverbild: www.ingimage.com

Verlag: VDM Verlag Dr. Müller Aktiengesellschaft & Co. KG
Dudweiler Landstr. 99, 66123 Saarbrücken, Deutschland
Telefon +49 681 9100-698, Telefax +49 681 9100-988
Email: info@vdm-verlag.de

Herstellung in Deutschland:
Schaltungsdienst Lange o.H.G., Berlin
Books on Demand GmbH, Norderstedt
Reha GmbH, Saarbrücken
Amazon Distribution GmbH, Leipzig
ISBN: 978-3-639-26110-3

Imprint (only for USA, GB)
Bibliographic information published by the Deutsche Nationalbibliothek: The Deutsche Nationalbibliothek lists this publication in the Deutsche Nationalbibliografie; detailed bibliographic data are available in the Internet at http://dnb.d-nb.de.

Any brand names and product names mentioned in this book are subject to trademark, brand or patent protection and are trademarks or registered trademarks of their respective holders. The use of brand names, product names, common names, trade names, product descriptions etc. even without a particular marking in this works is in no way to be construed to mean that such names may be regarded as unrestricted in respect of trademark and brand protection legislation and could thus be used by anyone.

Cover image: www.ingimage.com

Publisher: VDM Verlag Dr. Müller Aktiengesellschaft & Co. KG
Dudweiler Landstr. 99, 66123 Saarbrücken, Germany
Phone +49 681 9100-698, Fax +49 681 9100-988
Email: info@vdm-publishing.com

Printed in the U.S.A.
Printed in the U.K. by (see last page)
ISBN: 978-3-639-26110-3

Copyright © 2010 by the author and VDM Verlag Dr. Müller Aktiengesellschaft & Co. KG and licensors
All rights reserved. Saarbrücken 2010

Table of Contents

Introduction   7

PART ONE: THE NEED FOR STRATEGIC INNOVATION

1. The Nature of Strategic Management   13
2. The Need for New Concepts   21

PART TWO: STRATEGIC INNOVATION

3. What is Strategic Innovation?   31
4. The Content of Strategic Innovation   35
5. The Process of Strategic Innovation   85
6. The Context of Strategic Innovation   109
7. The Dimensions of Strategic Innovation   117

PART THREE: THE ROLE OF TOP MANAGEMENT

8. How to lead for Strategic Innovation   121

Conclusion   125

References   129

About the Author   141

Index of Figures

Figure 1 - Strategic Innovation and its Outcomes	33
Figure 2 - Strategy Dynamic	34
Figure 3 - The Content of Strategic Innovation	37
Figure 4 - Industries, Markets and Businesses	41
Figure 5 - Types of Firm Resources	46
Figure 6 - The Three Tiers of Noncustomers	48
Figure 7 - Shifting the Customer Value Frontier	58
Figure 8 - The Strategy Canvas of Southwest Airlines	60
Figure 9 - Redefining the Product: How to Identify New Products or Services?	62
Figure 10 - Elements of a Business Model	64
Figure 11 - Examples of Business Model Choices	64
Figure 12 - Elements of Hamel's Business Model	65
Figure 13 - Visualizing a Business Model	65
Figure 14 - Southwest Airlines' Activity System	75
Figure 15 - The Strategic Innovation Profile	83
Figure 16 - Types of Strategie	86
Figure 17 - Evaluating Ideas	101
Figure 18 - The Process of Strategic Innovation	105
Figure 19 - Rating your Company's Innovation Value Chain	107
Figure 20 - The Organizational Context of Strategic Innovation	111
Figure 21 - The Dimensions of Strategic Innovation	118

Index of Tables

Table 1 - Another Way of Saying "Mental Model"	39
Table 2 - Redefining the Market: Which Customers to Target?	52
Table 3 - Uncovering the Blocks to Buyer Utility	59
Table 4 - Redefining the Product: Dimensions and Tensions	62
Table 5 - The Nine Business Model Building Blocks	66
Table 6 - Assessing Distribution Channels	69
Table 7 - Redefining the Business Model	77
Table 8 - The Content Dimensions of Strategic Innovation	80
Table 9 - The Scale of the Strategic Innovation Profile	82
Table 10 - Idea Generation Techniques	91
Table 11 - The Ten Faces of Innovation	95
Table 12 - The Context Dimensions of Strategic Innovation	116

Acknowledgements

"It could be said of me that in this book I have only made up a bunch of other men's flowers, providing of my own only the string that ties them together."

(Montaigne)

As Montaigne, I have created a book that brings together many of the leading concepts, and ideas in the field of strategic innovation, synthesizing and arranging them into a comprehensive framework and making them more accessible to the interested reader.

In doing so, I am indebted to the many authors whose thinking I have used to compose this book.

I wish to thank my family for their continuous support in all my endeavors, for believing in me, giving me the energy and confidence to persist, and making pretty much everything possible.

Furthermore, I have to thank my colleagues at Doujak Corporate Development and especially Alexander and our clients for giving me the opportunity to test the ideas in this book in practice.

Finally, I am grateful to my wife, Danielle, for her love, patience and her encouragement in my moments of doubt.

Introduction

"Charles Darwin wrote a book on natural selection: Survival of the fittest, it turns out, is all about adapting to a changing environment and new competitive realities. That's exactly what companies face today – an uncertain business climate and disruptive technological changes. Your company's survival may depend on the way you answer one question: How will your company adapt?" (Judge 2001)

This introductory quote from the Fast Company issue of November 2001 summarizes the challenges that companies and their management still face today.

Business environments are changing faster than ever before, new technologies are emerging constantly at an increasing velocity, and industries are shaken by deregulations, mergers, new entrants and as we have recently seen unexpected world wide crises.

Some companies are able to adapt to these changing environments; others are not. What distinguishes the successful adapters, the "fittest", from the ones who fail? Why are some companies more successful than their competitors? Why do some companies achieve sustained high growth in both revenues and profits?

Besides the ability to sense shifts in their competitive environment (May, Anslinger et al. 2003), a crucial component of their success is their focus on strategy (Kaplan and Norton 2001; May, Anslinger et al. 2003), as well as a different view on strategic management (Kim and Mauborgne 1997; Markides 1999; Markides 1999) altogether. A view that does not solely rely on strategy as planning the next five years in terms of budget allocation or incremental efficiency improvements.

While these improvements might be necessary to compete in the market place, they are too short lived to gain a sustainable competitive advantage, which is absolutely necessary to ensure the survival of a company (Hamel 2001).

Successful companies have recognized that in order to be successful in the long run in terms of creating financial value and survival, they will need to achieve competitive advantage. And for these companies attaining competitive advantage is enabled through the creation of new markets, superior customer value, new business models and disruptive innovation. They have also recognized that, as every competitive advantage is only sustainable for a limited period of time, doing this once is not enough; theses companies know that their organization needs to build the capabilities necessary for ongoing strategic innovation (Brown 2002). As Christensen (2001) points out "...today's competitive advantage may become tomorrow's albatross...".

In addition there is strong evidence that successfully innovative companies are more likely to generate superior growth rates (Ziegler 2002).

The question arising is, how a company can achieve such ongoing strategic innovation, leading to competitive advantage and financial success?

Although managers might know that innovation is the only way to attain competitive advantage, they seldom know where to begin (Kim and Mauborgne 1999).

Unfortunately more often than not the advice that companies should be prepared to be more innovative and "think outside the box", if they want to develop innovative strategies and remain successful, is rarely accompanied by helpful steps on how to accomplish this (Kreuz 2001).

Furthermore during the last couple of years a number of different theories have been developed around the theme of strategic innovation, with several authors having provided only partial solutions (Loewe, Williamson et al. 2001), making it exceedingly difficult to retain an overview. This is even reinforced by the variety of ways to achieve strategic innovation (Mang 2000; Sawhney, Wolcott et al. 2006).

And with growth driven by innovation being on the top of managers' agendas throughout the world again (Carden, Mendonca et al. 2005; Smit, Thompson et al. 2005), knowing how to achieve it is now more important than ever.

Objectives of this book

The primary objective of this book is, from a theoretical point of view, to (1) summaries and structure the current research and theories and, to (2) synthesize these insights and partial solutions from different authors into a comprehensive approach facilitating a systematic way for thinking through the issues involved.

In addition, from a managerial point of view, the aim is to (3) provide a practical framework and advice that will help managers think about how to develop and implement innovative strategies, capable of creating sustainable competitive advantage and describe concrete approaches to enable this process, while keeping in mind that "the beast of strategy formation" consists of different perspectives and that practicing managers have to deal with the entire beast and not just parts of it (Mintzberg and Lampel 1999; Markides 2001).

Structure of the book

In order to achieve the above-cited objectives the book is organized in 5 parts.

- **Part 1** analyses (1) the aim and nature of strategic management, and presents (2) criticism about the way strategic management is handled today, which will lead us to the need for new concepts.
- **Part 2** will focus on providing a sound grounding on what it means to be strategically innovative and synthesizes the current theories into a systematic approach.

    According to De Wit and Meyer (2004) strategy problems can be categorized along the three dimensions (1) content, (2) process, and (3) context. They argue that the advantage of such an issue-based structure and approach to thinking about strategy is that it is problem-driven, and decision-oriented instead of focusing too much on the tools, or a certain perspective.

    Markides (2000) follows a similar categorization, when he explains that in order to develop a strategy, we first have to ask ourselves certain questions (i.e. content), and then find creative answers, make choices, and implement the resulting strategies (i.e. process), in a given environment or context.

    This problem-driven approach, used for structuring part 3, will enable us to have a holistic look at the issues of strategic innovation, taking various aspects and perspectives into account, instead of following a step-by-step, single tool driven approach.

    Hence, in part three, (1) a *definition* of strategic innovation will be provided, followed by (2) a presentation of a comprehensive approach to the *content* of strategic innovation synthesizing different theories, as well as (3) a description of the *process* of strategy formation in general and of innovative strategies in particular. Finally, this part will close with a presentation of the (4) *context* of strategic innovation, while focusing primarily on the organizational context and describing characteristics of strategically innovative companies.

- **Part 3** analyses the managerial implications, especially the role of top management in leading strategic innovation.

Part One
The Need for Strategic Innovation

The first part aims at showing the need for a new perspective on strategy.

- First, a brief overview of the current discussion concerning the creation and content of strategies will be summarized from the literature and common elements will be elaborated.
- This will be followed by a description of strategic management in companies today, and an explanation of why this practice is not suited to fulfill the tasks of strategic management, which will lead us to the need for new concepts.

1. The Nature of Strategic Management

"Nobody really knows what strategy is."

(Economist March, 20 1993)

Although strategy has an obvious importance in business and despite a lot of academic research on the topic, and the general agreement that every company needs a strategy, there is little agreement on what a strategy really is or how to develop a good one (Mintzberg 1987; Camillus 1996; Markides 1999; 2000; Kaplan and Norton 2001; De Wit and Meyer 2004), there are no straightforward definitions or rules, there is no "widespread agreement among practitioners, researchers and theorists as to what strategy is" (De Wit and Meyer 2004).

Mintzberg (1999) identified ten schools of thought on strategy formation: Design School, Planning School, Positioning School, Entrepreneurial School, Cognitive School, Learning School, Power School, Cultural School, Environmental School, Configuration School, and argues that these represent different approaches to strategy formation, as well as different stages of the same process. Nevertheless, they all help to gain a better understanding of strategic management as a whole.

In his earlier work Mintzberg (1987) offered five definitions of strategy, namely strategy as:

(1) A consciously and purposefully developed plan;

(2) A ploy to outmaneuver a competitor;

(3) A pattern in a stream of actions, whether intended or not;

(4) A position defined either with respect to a competitor, in the context of a number of competitors, or with respect to markets; and as

(5) A perspective, i.e. a certain mindset of how to perceive the world.

Markides (2001) reasons that regarding to the content of strategy, there are two main schools:

(1) The view of strategy that emphasizes the positioning elements; and

(2) The more dynamic view, which emphasizes outplaying and out-maneuvering competitors.

While the first seems to be about "choosing a game to play" the second is about "how to play it". He concludes that strategy, of course, is both of these. It must decide what game to play, as well as determine how to play it (Eisenhardt 1999; Markides 2001).

Furthermore Markides (2001) describes that regarding to the process of strategy there is also a lot of disagreement. Can a strategy be planned or does it emerge? Where do we start our analysis? Do we start the process by analyzing the market or by focusing on our existing competencies?

De Wit and Meyer (2004) as well as Davenport (Davenport, Leibold et al. 2006), reason that every real-life strategic problem has three dimensions, namely the strategy process, the strategy content, and the strategy context, and that every dimension features several issues, which have to be taken into account, while every issue again is characterized by certain fundamental tensions and oppositional viewpoints, both in theory and practice.

As for the **process**, they identify three topics, which all bear their own tension:

(1) Strategic thinking, which can be logical or creative,
(2) Strategy formation, which can be deliberate or emergent,
(3) Strategic change, which can be revolutionary or evolutionary.

As for the **content**, again three distinct issues can be approached from different sides:

(1) Business level strategy, can be viewed from a perspective focusing on the market or on the company's resources,
(2) Corporate level strategy, can focus either on responsiveness or synergy,
(3) Network level strategy, can be competitive or cooperative.

When it comes to the **context**, paradoxes in regard to:

(1) The industry context, can range from compliance to choice,
(2) The organization context, from control to chaos,
(3) The international context, from globalization to localization.

A McKinsey study found three sources of sound strategy development (Gluck, Kaufman et al. 2000):

(1) Strategic thinking (creative, entrepreneurial, insight into a company, its industry and its environment)

(2) Formal strategic planning (systematic, comprehensive approaches to developing strategies)
(3) Opportunistic strategic decision-making (effective responses to unexpected opportunities and problems).

Again, all three are different approaches and anyone can lead to a good strategy.

Porter (McCarthy 2000) and Grant (2002) argue that an analytical approach is best for strategy development, while Mintzberg (1993) counters that strategy formation is not about analysis, but about synthesis. Ohmae (1982) and Markides (2001) add that it is creativity, which gives great strategies an extraordinary competitive impact, while Liedtka (2000) favors strategy as design.

Despite these disagreements about what a strategy is or how to develop a good one there are certain similarities and shared beliefs.

The purpose of strategy is competitive advantage

A great many researchers and practitioners (Ohmae 1982; 1982; 1982; Porter 1985; Ohmae 1988; Henderson 1989; Hinterhuber 1989; Barney 1991; Grant 1991; Hinterhuber and Popp 1992; Hoffmann, Klien et al. 1996; Coyne, Buaron et al. 2000; Koch 2000; Mang 2000; Markides 2000; Hammonds 2001; Cool, Costa et al. 2002; Grant 2002) have pointed out that "a fundamental question in the strategic management field is how companies achieve and sustain competitive advantage" (Cool, Costa et al. 2002).

Grant (2002) defines competitive advantage as follows: "When two or more firms compete within the same market, one firm possesses a competitive advantage over its rival when it earns (or has the potential to earn) a persistently higher rate of profit" (Grant 2002), and thereby links the outcome of competitive advantage directly to the financial performance and profitability of a company, which Porter (Hammonds 2001), Kaplan and Norton (2001), as well as Coyne, Buaron et al. (2000) and Demos, Chung et al. (2001) also consider being the ultimate goal of strategy.

Coyne, Buaron et al. (2000), as well as Hinterhuber and Popp (1992) define competitive advantage as customers choosing to buy from a certain company instead of from its competitors. This choice arises from the fact that the customers "perceive a consistent difference between the company's product or service and those of its competition, and that difference must occur in one or more key buying criteria" (Coyne, Buaron et al. 2000), a reasoning shared with Hinterhuber and Popp (1992).

Competitive advantage can emerge from a variety of sources, which can be classified as belonging to two distinct categories:

(1) The **resource-based view**, emphasizing the importance of specific resources and capabilities owned by a company, (e.g. specific core competencies, or greater creative and innovative capabilities), or

(2) Privileged **market positions** as a source of competitive advantage resulting from a certain industry structure in which competitors have no incentive to imitate the leader.

If the competitive advantages arises from changes in the external market environment, the company still needs the necessary internal capabilities to cope with these changes and respond effectively (Grant 2002).

But, no matter what view a company pursues, competitive advantage means to be better than your competitors, and "...doing better, by definition, means being different" (Magretta 2002).

Strategy is about being different

"I don't think there's anything worse than being ordinary."

(American Beauty, the movie)

"A sustainable competitive advantage begins with a unique capability that shields a company from competition" (Coyne, Buaron et al. 2000).

The key to successful strategic management is to create as much differentiation as possible and diverge from competitors by occupying unique strategic positions, which are necessary for a company's success and that no competitor can match or approach (Porter 1985; Henderson 1989; Hinterhuber and Popp 1992; Eschenbach and Kunesch 1996; Porter 1996; Eisenhardt 1999; Harari 1999; Markides 1999; Koch 2000; Markides 2000; Peters 2000; Eisenhardt and Sull 2001; Hammonds 2001; Kim and Mauborgne 2002; Hamel and Välikangas 2003).

Henderson (1989) goes even so far as to say that a business has no reason to exist, unless it has a unique advantage over its competitors. He reasons that according to

Gause's[1] principal of competitive advantage, competitors, which are too similar, cannot exist in the same space. Each must be different enough to have a unique advantage.

Uniqueness, enabling competitive advantage, can emerge from a variety of sources, like for instance:

- A business system allowing a company to perform a function better, and above all, different than competitors (Porter 1996; Coyne, Buaron et al. 2000; Markides 2000);
- A distinct position in the market or a specific target segment (Porter 1996; Coyne, Buaron et al. 2000; Markides 2000), which might be only the customers' perception and the image she has of the company (Henderson 1989);
- Governmental regulations or laws (e.g. import quotas, patents, etc.) (Porter 1985; Coyne, Buaron et al. 2000);
- Organizational or managerial competencies, resulting from the organization's ability to innovate or adept more quickly and effectively (Grant 1991; Coyne, Buaron et al. 2000; Hamel and Välikangas 2003).

No matter where the differentiation arises from, it is the basis of a company's advantage and strategy is the "deliberate search for a plan of action that will develop a business's competitive advantage" (Henderson 1989).

Strategy is about making choices

"The most common source of strategic failure is the failure to make clear and explicit choices."

(Markides 2000)

A company cannot be everything to everyone; resources are limited and therefore choices on how to use them have to be made (Itami 1987; Kreilkamp 1987; Drucker 1993; Porter 1996; Markides 1999; 2000; Eisenhardt and Sull 2001; Hammonds 2001). It is the task of strategic management to do so and thereby "...enable the organization to concentrate its resources and exploit its opportunities and its own existing skills and knowledge to the very fullest" (Mintzberg 1987).

---

[1] G.F. Gause's Priniciple of Competitive Exclusion: No two species can coexist that make their living in an identical way.

Furthermore Kim and Mauborgne (2002), Ohmae (1982), Clemons and Santamaria (2002), Mintzberg (1987), Pearson (2002), Joyce, Nohria et al. (2003) as well as Ogilvy (2003) and a recent Accenture study (Breene and Nues 2005) argue that an element of good strategy is its focus. If a company wants to focus, it has to take decisions and make clear strategic choices.

Choices are not limited to the usage of resources though. It is also a question of strategic positions, which market segments to address, setting direction and which activities to perform (Mintzberg 1987; Henderson 1989; Hinterhuber and Popp 1992). All these choices necessitate certain trade-offs.

According to Porter (1996) trade-offs arise for three reasons. They can occur from:

(1) Inconsistencies in image or reputation. A company known for delivering one kind of value will not be able to credibly deliver another kind of value.

(2) The activities themselves. Different activities require different product configurations, different equipment, different skills, etc. The more a company might focus on lowering costs, the less able it is to satisfy customers requiring a higher service level for example.

(3) Limits on internal coordination and control. The choice of competing in one way and not another defines organizational priorities. If companies try to be all things to all customers, they risk confusing the customers, as well as the employees when they have to take day-to-day decisions.

We could add that trade-offs also occur from the simple fact that time, money and increasingly talent can be scarce in organizations and everyday life. Choices on how to allocate them have to be made and trade-offs accepted.

When making choices (what issues have to be decided upon will be discussed in the coming chapters), it is important to keep in mind that they do not only define which activities to perform and how to configure individual ones, but also how activities relate to one another.

Strategy has to fit

A final important point is that a strategy and the choices a company makes need to fit, both internally and externally.

McKinsey defines strategy as "an integrated set of actions designed to create a sustainable competitive advantage" (Coyne, Buaron et al. 2000), while according to Porter "strategy is about combining activities" (Porter 1996).

First all the activities carried out by a company have to reinforce each other and together build a system (Porter 1996; Markides 2000; Kaplan and Norton 2001).

Not only does a system of activities make it easier to achieve competitive advantage, it also creates a more sustainable one. While individual activities might be relatively easy to be copied by competitors, it is much harder to do so with a complete system (Porter 1996; Markides 2000).

Second, not only have the activities within a company to fit, but they do also have to correspond to the organization's environment; the activities carried out have to be the ones demanded by the market (Markides 1999; 2000). There needs to be a fit between the internal strengths and weaknesses and the external threats and opportunities (Mintzberg and Lampel 1999).

The aim of strategy

According to the explanations given above, throughout this book the aim of strategic management will be defined as enabling competitive advantage through differentiation and acquiring a unique position in the market, as well as the customers' perception, by making explicit choices and aligning the company's activities and resources in relation to each other and the market's needs.

The questions that arise are:

(1) Whether strategic management as practiced in companies today is appropriate to attain competitive advantage through differentiation?

(2) Whether the traditional strategic management tools are still suited to do so; and if not;

(3) How such differentiation and competitive advantage, leading to superior long-term financial success, can be achieved?

2. The Need for New Concepts

"There's no good just being better,... you got to be different!"

(Charles Handy at the London Business Forum 2002)

What follows is a summary of the criticism by leading academics, as well as practicing managers, about the way strategic management functions in companies today and the traditional approaches to strategy. This criticism can be organized along three distinct categories:

(1) The **content** of strategic management, i.e. what does strategy focus on?

(2) The **process** of strategic management, i.e. how are new strategies developed?

(3) And finally the **tools** used for strategic management.

Criticism of the content

"...pursuing incremental improvements while rivals reinvent the industry is like fiddling while Rome burns."

(Hamel 1996)

The criticism as regard to the content of current strategy practice revolves around three main themes: (1) focusing on best practice and operational effectiveness (2) too much imitation of competitors' moves and (3) finding and holding one strategic position. As we will see the three themes are closely related to each other and interleaved and thus will be discussed simultaneously.

As discussed above the ultimate aim of strategy is competitive advantage through differentiation, which will enable a company to be successful from a financial perspective.

Financial success can be measured in a number of ways. Usually a whole array of ratios, like Profitability, Return on Sales, Return on Investment, Return on Equity, Return on Capital Employed, or Value Management concepts, like Economic Value Added, Cash

Value Added, or some customized variations of these, or other concepts, are at a company's disposal to do so. A common element of all these concepts, and a so-called value driver in general, is profit (or again some variation of profit, e.g. EBIT, EBITDA, NOPAT, etc.). It is not only a vital indicator, as well as a measure, of financial success, but profit is also absolutely necessary to ensure the survival of any given company.

Profits being the result of revenues minus costs, it can only be raised in two ways: either we increase the revenues or we decrease the costs. In recent years management has mainly be engaged in the reduction of costs (Hamel 2001), and improved operational effectiveness (Markides 2000; Davenport, Leibold et al. 2006) through such techniques as scientific management, operations research, reengineering, enterprise resource planning, Six Sigma, etc. (Hamel 2001; Hamel and Välikangas 2003).

Although such optimizations and improvements are necessary and have produced a considerable amount of wealth, they are hardly enough and do not lead to much differentiation and superior financial success (Lynn, Morone et al. 1996; Godin 2001; Hammonds 2001; Hamel and Välikangas 2003).

According to Porter (Porter 1996; Hammonds 2001) the origin of the problem stems from the failure to distinguish between operational effectiveness and strategy. He defines operational effectiveness as performing similar activities better than your competition, while strategic positioning is about performing similar activities different, not only better, or performing different activities altogether. Hamel (1998), as well as Nattermann (1999) agree by saying that operational efficiency and getting better is not a strategy.

Operational effectiveness might be necessary to achieve superior profitability and survive in the market, but concentrating only on productivity leads to doing the same thing than the competitors, which in turn leads to a rapprochement of competitors and their strategies (Porter 1996; Hamel 2001; Kim and Mauborgne 2002) and not the necessary differentiation.

Furthermore such a focus on operational effectiveness misleads companies to assessing what their peers do, matching and copying their every move and striving for doing more of it, doing it better, faster and cheaper (Ohmae 1988; Kim and Mauborgne 1997; Kim and Mauborgne 1999; Kim and Mauborgne 1999; Hamel 2001; Hamel and Välikangas 2003).

Too much focus on what competitors do and trying to do it better in turn leads to reactive and only incremental improvements in cost or quality or both (Hamel and Prahalad 1989;

Hamel and Prahalad 1997; Kim and Mauborgne 1997; 1999; Nattermann 1999; Hammonds 2001), rather than to the creation of sustainable competitive advantages.

As a result companies do not differentiate themselves anymore, but compete against each other only along the same lines and basic dimensions of competition (Kim and Mauborgne 1999; Nattermann 1999; Hamel and Välikangas 2003): costs, operational effectiveness and price (Hamel 2001). This lack of strategic differentiation leaves customers choosing on price only, which in turn results in collapsing margins within an industry (Kim and Mauborgne 1999; 1999; Nattermann 1999; Hammonds 2001; Hamel and Välikangas 2003; Kim and Mauborgne 2004; 2005).

Several McKinsey studies (Nattermann 1999) have supported this view. One study for example showed that imitation of best practices in the German mobile telecom industry lead to a decline in strategic differentiation of 83 percent accompanied by a 50 percent decrease of margins between 1992 and 1998.

The industry leader in such a position might even face another problem: the "herding phenomenon". According to Nattermann (1999) the above described imitation of competitors by copying best practices leads to a clustering of companies around the most successful one, which destroys value, as the profits of the leader are soon to be divided among the group of companies converging around its space.

This problem is even reinforced by the fact that most companies take their current position and practices as given and do not even question long-established industry rules. They share a common set of beliefs on how to compete in a certain industry or strategic group (Kim and Mauborgne 1999; Markides 2000; Kim and Mauborgne 2004; 2005), which leads them to protect and improve their gained strategic position paying little attention to searching for or discovering new ones in the market (Markides 2000).

Instead of trying to set themselves apart and escape from the herd, once companies have found a strategy that works, or has worked in the past, they want to use it, not change it. As a consequence companies are unable to see the need for change when the strategy that made them great has become obsolete (Christensen 1997; Demos, Chung et al. 2001).

Criticism of the process

The criticism as regard to the process of current strategy practice revolves around two main themes: (1) strategic planning usually being nothing more than an incremental adaptation of last year's plan, and (2) the planning process being too formal and analytical. Again, these themes are closely related to each other and thus will be discussed together.

Criticism of strategic management, as it is practiced today, comes from various authors (Hamel and Prahalad 1989; Mintzberg 1994; Camillus 1996; Hamel 1996; Hamel and Prahalad 1997; Yates and Skarzynski 1999; Hamel 2001; Beinhocker and Kaplan 2002) who argue that the process of strategy development in companies today is rather the continuation and incremental adaptation of last year's plans and budgets, than the search for new opportunities and differentiation. This also relates to the above stated argument that companies, once they have found a strategy, or position that has been successful in the past, are not willing to change.

Furthermore, strategic planning is often a very formal and analytical process by which standardized forms are filled in by various departments and business units and then reported back to central planning. This standardized process leaves no room for adaptation to new markets, developments and opportunities and it is argued that real strategic decisions are not made in the context of a formal process (Mintzberg 1987; Beinhocker and Kaplan 2003; Mankins 2004).

As this process usually is repeated only once a year it is also argued that in today's fast-cycle environments, by the time all the documents have been filled in, reported and the final plan has been published and distributed, the environment is likely to have changed and the plan to be outdated (Camillus 1998; Mankins 2004).

Another point raising criticism is the fact that traditional strategic planning is seen as an analytical process only (Roos 2004; Davenport, Leibold et al. 2006). The process takes the form of mindless number crunching the purpose of which is to create huge reports that probably nobody even reads (Markides 2001). But planning and analysis do not lead to a strategy (Mintzberg 1987; Hamel and Prahalad 1989; Hamel 1996; 1998; Eisenhardt 1999; Markides 2001). They rather lead to the above-mentioned incremental changes of last year's plan.

Liedtka (2000) adds that this view of strategy usually focuses on a single technique inappropriately applied and entails a loss of creativity. An argument supported by Mintzberg (1987; 1993; 1994) and Markides (2000; 2001).

Additionally this formalized planning process, usually coming from the top, raises little commitment from front line managers (Bartlett and Ghoshal 1994), as the need for upward communication is ignored (Hamel and Prahalad 1989). Thus strategy processes are often disconnected from the realities of the market place because of personal, political and institutional factors and usually there is little alignment between strategic goals and resource allocation (Christensen 1997).

We could add to this that planning is nothing more than a mere shot in the dark, a feeble attempt to master and control the future by creating the illusion that it can by foreseen (Mintzberg 1993; Sanders 1998; Harari 1999). And as we all should know, this can simply not be done. This obsession with control leads to a certain reluctance to consider truly creative ideas and changes, as the outcome of both are unpredictable and thereby beyond formal planning (Mintzberg 1993; Krinsky and Jenkins 1997). As the saying goes, "a plan is all the things that do not happen".

Davenport, Leibold et al (2006) highlight further deficiencies, namely the assumption of linearity of the strategy process, which usually consists of strategy analysis, formulation, implementation, and change. In practice, they argue, the process is rather diffuse with these elements ongoing and intertwining.

Criticism of the tools

The last set of criticism one can observe in the literature centers around the tools used in strategic management, with the arguments mainly underlining the focus of the tools, just like the process, being to analytical and oriented towards planning.

A historic look at the evolution of strategic management shows that at the beginning corporate planning was associated with the problems faced by managers in the 1950s and 1960s. As their companies grew larger and became more complex they were in the need of tools, techniques, and systems for maintaining control. Annual budgets were among the first tools developed, followed by long-term (usually five year) plans for coordinating capital investment decisions and taking advantage of economies of scale, largely based on economic and market forecasts. The desire to grow and changes in the market place (e.g. the oil shocks of 1974 and 1979) led to new techniques like for example Ansoff's SWOT analysis, or Porter's Five Forces, which are mainly analytical in nature, and again focused on mastering and controlling the environment. The tools might have become more sophisticated, but the goals remained the same: master and control, by analyzing the environment and planning your course of action.

Considering that the tools used in strategic management today are still the ones that were developed during these years, or at least still remain grounded in the analysis and planning philosophy, we might argue that strategic management is weighted down by its historic baggage.

Thus the argument that there is a large gap between what managers want to achieve today, competitive advantage through differentiation, and what the traditional tools were developed for, analysis and planning (Amram and Kulatilaka 1999; Demos, Chung et al. 2001; Davenport, Leibold et al. 2006).

What's more, not only the purpose of strategic management is no longer the one the tools were developed for but also the circumstances under which they were created are no longer the same (Hamel 1998; Roos 2004). According to Coyne and Subramaniam (1996) 50 percent of strategic problems faced by companies today lie outside the conditions for which the traditional model was designed. Sanders (1998) adds that the strategy models are too complicated, take too long, are too inflexible and disconnected from the dynamics of the real world and not suited to understand its complexities.

Traditional competitor analysis is primarily occupied with monitoring existing competitors, products and markets (Hamel and Prahalad 1989; Harari 1999), while we have seen a lot of new entrants, new products and new markets developing in recent years. In addition, as Christensen (1997) has shown the most successful products are not necessarily launched by industry leaders.

Traditional market research revolves around existing customer needs and mind-sets, although very often the customer herself might not know what she could possibly want and very often customers say one thing and act in a completely different way. Lynn (Lynn, Morone et al. 1996) even shows that the use of these tools is no critical factor in the decision making process leading to innovations.

Courtney (2001) explains while traditional tools like Porter's Five-Forces may provide insight, they do not generally generate a lot of foresight, which is needed to create creative strategies for the future. Mintzberg and Lampel (1999) add that these analytical tools do not create strategy as intended by Porter, as they only offer insights which can be used in thinking about what strategy to pursue. Hambrick and Fredrickson (2001) add that these tools only focus on the input of strategy.

Kim and Mauborgne (2005) argue that the traditional view, and thereby the tools used, of strategy focuses too much on competing in existing market space, beating the competition, exploit existing demand, making the value/cost trade off, and aligning the whole system of a company's activities with its strategic choice of differentiation or low cost.

And finally: Some organizations use planning tools, not because anyone inside the company necessarily believes in them but simply, because influential outsiders do, utilizing them rather for public relations purposes than real strategic management (Mintzberg 1993).

This criticism of the traditional approaches, tools and techniques – strategy as operational effectiveness, as an analytical and incremental process focusing too much on beating the competition and defending a maybe outdated strategic position by using tools that were not invented for the problems at hand – leads to the assumption that strategic management, as it is practiced by companies today, is not suited to gain a unique position in the market, a position, which enables a company to build and sustain lasting competitive advantages and guarantee the necessary success and streams of revenues to assure the long term survival of a company.

Because of this criticism and the disadvantages described above, new approaches to strategic management have been developed. Regrouped under the term "Strategic Innovation" they represent a new way of thinking about strategy and offer new approaches to the development of strategies that enable a company to attain such differentiation, which is necessary for competitive advantage. These new approaches are as much about new tools and new processes, as about a completely new mindset, when it comes to thinking strategically.

Part Two
Strategic Innovation

"...those who live by the sword will be shot by those who don't."

(Gary Hamel)

Part two will answer the question of what a company has to do if it intends to develop and implement an innovative strategy, which will enable it to create sustaining competitive advantage.

- First a definition of strategic innovation will be elaborated (chapter 3).
- Next, the content of strategic innovation, i.e. the issues that have to be thought through will be summarized from the literature and synthesized into a comprehensive approach helping managers not only to ask the right questions but also providing insight on where to find answers to these questions (chapter 4).
- Chapter 5 describes the process of strategic innovation and provides a number of tools and techniques on how to find answers to the questions raised before and will be followed by
- A description of the characteristics of strategically innovative companies, enabling continuous innovation (chapter 6).

3. What is Strategic Innovation?

To develop a definition of strategic innovation it is useful to consider a number of views and then extract a generic description.

- Hamel and Prahalad (1989) write about strategic intent enabling a company to create new industry space and core competencies facilitating the invention of new markets (Hamel and Prahalad 1990).
- Markides (1997; 1998; 1999; 2000) defines strategic innovation as a fundamentally different way of competing in an industry by breaking the rules of the game and thinking of new ways to compete. A major element to him is the "...fundamental reconceptualization of what the business is about, which in turn leads to a dramatically different way of playing the game in the industry" (Markides 2000).
- Krinsky and Jenksins (1997) talk about the use of creativity and innovation to break the rules in order to attain competitive advantage.
- Tushman (1997) explains that the ability to manage disruptive, as well as incremental, streams of innovation leads to new markets and the rewriting of industry rules.
- Kim and Mauborgne (1997; 1999) write about "value innovation" as a new strategic logic making the competition irrelevant by offering fundamentally new and superior value in existing markets or enabling the creation of new markets through quantum leaps in value for both the buyer and the company itself (Kim and Mauborgne 2005).
- Hamel (1998; 1998) states that strategy innovation is the capacity to reconceive the existing industry model in ways that create new value for customers, wrong-foot competitors and produce new wealth for all stakeholders by devising a product or service, redefining the market space, or redrawing industry boundaries (Hamel 1996). He also points out that key competitive advantage arises from innovation in

- the business model itself (Hamel 1998; Hamel 2001), the goal of business model innovation being to create a larger strategic diversity in the market and competitive environment (Hamel 2001).

- Yates and Skarzynski (1999) talk of strategy innovation being about rethinking the basis of competition for any company in any industry. In particular, they mention inventing new business models and breaking through traditional boundaries to create new market spaces.

- Christensen, Johnson et al (2002) talk about disruptive innovation resulting "...in the creation of entirely new markets and business models" and that growth comes from new ways of competing.

- Markides and Charitou (2003) define strategic innovation as "innovation in one's business model that leads to a new way of playing the game" and strategic innovators as companies attacking "the established players by using radical different business models" (Markides and Charitou 2004).

- Hamel and Välikangas talk about resilience as "... the ability to dynamically reinvent business models and strategies as circumstances change" (Hamel and Välikangas 2003).

- According to Govindarajan and Trimble (2004) "strategic innovation is a creative and significant departure from historical practice in at least one of three areas: the design of the end-to-end value chain architecture, the conceptualization of delivered customer value, or the identification of potential customers."

- Govindarajan and Gupta (2001) identified three arenas for changing the rules of the game: dramatically redesign the end-to-end value chain, the concept of customer value, or the customer base.

- Geroski (1998) views the redefinition of and thinking creatively about a market by introducing new products or addressing the needs of new customers as the key to strategic innovation.

The outcomes of strategic innovation

Considering these definitions, three outcomes of strategic innovation can be identified. Strategic innovation leads to either

  (1) New **business models** (including a new value chain architecture), or
  (2) New **markets** (either by creating new ones or reshaping existing ones), or
  (3) Increased **value** for both the customer and the company

or a combination of these three.

Drawing upon the above said, strategic innovation will be defined as:

- A framework of interdependent content, process and context dimensions,
- facilitating the application of creativity and innovation to strategic management
- in order to enable strategic differentiation and competitive advantage,
- by challenging conventional logic and redefining the company's business model, redrawing market boundaries, creating new markets and value improvements for customers and the company itself.

Figure 1 illustrates the sequence and outcomes of strategic innovation.

Strategic Innovation
- Content
- Process
- Context

New Way of Playing the Game
- New Business Models
- New Markets
- Value Improvements

Differentiation
- New Strategic Position

Competitive Advantage

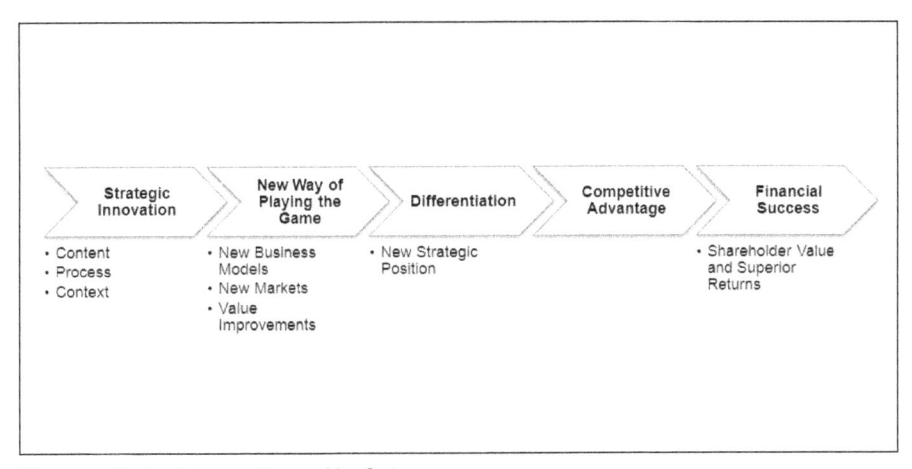

Financial Success
- Shareholder Value and Superior Returns

Figure 1 - Strategic Innovation and its Outcomes

To illustrate the concept of strategic innovation, we can use Chakravarthy and White's (2002) strategy dynamics graph (Figure 2). According to them innovation goes beyond established best practices and advances the strategy frontier, represented by the curved solid line, where those firms with the current best practices are positioned.

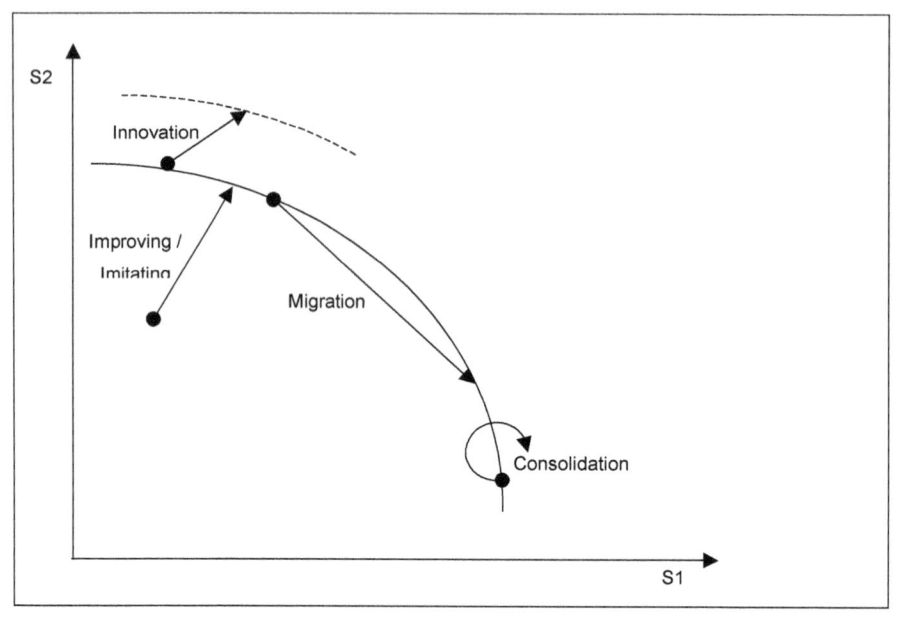

Figure 2 - Strategy Dynamic (Chakravarthy and White 2002)

The question arising now is how this new way of playing the game can be achieved. How can companies advance the strategy frontier? How can managers think about the issues involved in a systematic way and identify opportunities for creating new business models, new markets, or deliver quantum leaps in value for their company and their customers?

4. The Content of Strategic Innovation

"Effective strategic thinking is the process of continually asking questions and thinking through the issues in a creative way."

(Markides 2000 p. ix)

As described above the criticism of strategic management's content revolves around companies focusing too much on being better than their competition instead of trying to be different. This chapter will outline the content dimensions of strategic innovation and related issues that have to be thought thru and considered while developing an innovative strategy. The content dimensions are meant to guide the thinking process by offering a structure and directions for shifting the focus from conventional logic to strategic innovation.

Many authors (Abell 1980; Kim and Mauborgne 1997; Markides 1997; Markides 1998; Wells 1998; Kim and Mauborgne 1999; Markides 1999; Markides 1999; Markides 1999; Yates and Skarzynski 1999; Koch 2000; Markides 2000; De Wit and Meyer 2004) underline the importance of asking questions in order to challenge the status quo of industry rules and the basis of competition as a starting point for developing breakthrough strategies and strategy in general.

This chapter will deal with what questions to ask and suggest directions for finding answers.

In the strategy literature "strategy content" usually relates to business level strategy, corporate level strategy, network level strategy and occasionally also functional level strategy (for example De Wit and Meyer (2004), Grant (2002), or Pettigrew, Thomas et al. (2002)).

The concepts of strategic innovation presented here can mainly be applied to the business level, although certain aspects definitely will have implications on the various functions and even on the larger network or ecosystem, the company is imbedded in.

Abell (1980) describes that defining the business is the starting point of strategy and suggests the three dimensions: costumer groups, customer function, and technology to do so. Although Abell did not write about strategic innovation explicitly, he mentioned that existing market boundaries will be reshaped once the business of a company has been redefined along these three dimensions, his argument being that the "individual business definition determines market boundary definition" (Abell 1980) and not, as conventional wisdom would suggest, the other way round.

Markides (1997; 1999; 1999; 1999; 2000), drawing on Abell's work, explains that a company's strategy is above all defined by the answers to the four questions,

(1) What business are you in?

(2) Who should be your customer?

(3) What products or services should you offer?

(4) How should this be done?

A similar approach is chosen by Drucker (1994), who refers to the answers and assumptions regarding the aspects of what is your business, who is your customer, what technology to use, what does the customer consider value, what is the company's plan, as a company's theory of business and uses these questions to asses organizations (Drucker 1993).

Hamel mentions that companies need "...to be able to ask themselves the fundamental questions – who are we and how do we compete, which customers do we serve, what are we doing..." (Hamel 1998).

Camillus (1996) talks about "dimensions of strategic choice" and refers to the type of client the organization would serve, sources of revenue, the basis for diversification, and the kind of technology relevant to the organization.

Govindarajan and Gupta (2001) argue that a business model results from answering the three questions:

(1) Who are my target customers?

(2) What value do I want to deliver to them?

(3) How will I create it?

As we shall see the thinking and theories of other writers also fit into the "who-what-how" framework and offer further going questions helping managers to gain deeper insights and finding creative and innovative answers.

Figure 3 outlines the general content dimensions of strategic innovation. We will discuss each of these questions separately starting with the overall question of what business the company is in, followed by "Who's the customer", "What product to offer" and "How to do this", the aim being not simply to ask these questions but to redefine the company's current answers.

The chapter will close with a summary of these dimensions and their sub elements and the development of a tool for mapping strategic innovation.

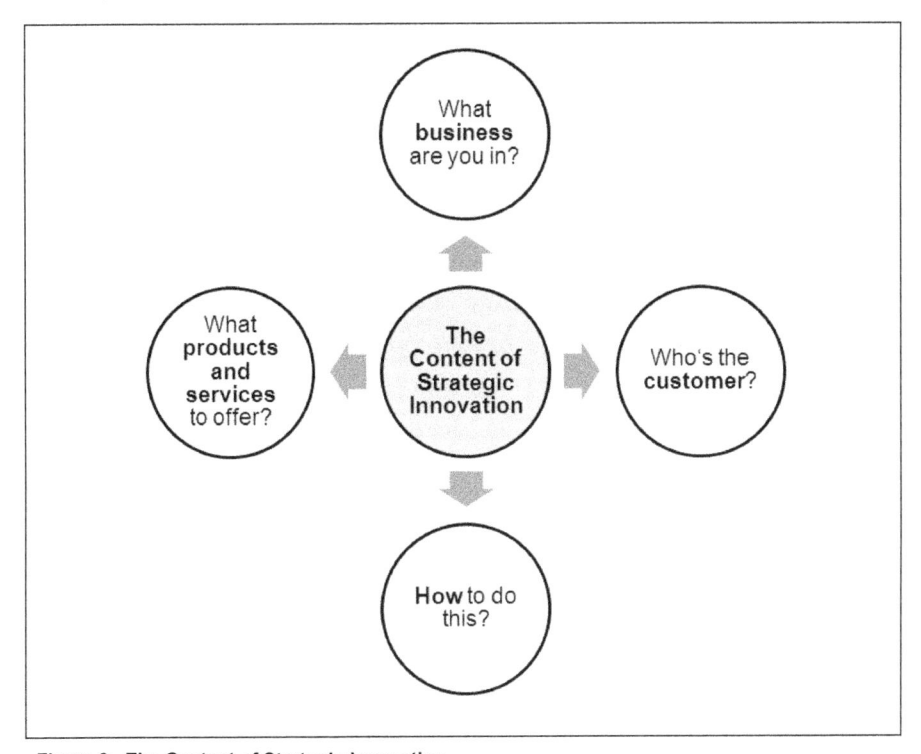

Figure 3 - The Content of Strategic Innovation

Redefining the business

"Starbucks is not in the coffee business."

(Howard Schultz, Chairman Starbucks Inc.)

The starting point of strategic innovation is questioning the perception of what business the company believes to be in. Although it might seem a bit odd, the importance of asking this question lies in the answer defining the way the organization thinks about its customers, people, processes, products, and competitors. Furthermore Frazier and Howell (1983) have shown that variations in business definitions have an impact on performance.

What business a company beliefs to be in defines who it considers as its customers, its competitors, what it thinks the success factors of the industry are and "...thus ultimately determines how it plays the game" (Markides 1997).

Markides (1997; 2000) refers to the behavior of an organization, as well as an individual, as being defined by its "mental models", while Hinterhuber (1996) talks about "corporate policy" defining the intended purpose and scope of business activities.

Kim and Mauborgne (1999) write about companies sharing a "conventional wisdom", a set of beliefs about how to compete in an industry or in a strategic group.

Bower (2003) writes that "the way we do things around here" is determined by the company's philosophy, while De Wit and Meyer refer to "cognitive maps" as "representations in a person's mind of how the world works" (De Wit and Meyer 2004).

Drucker writes about a company's theory of business as the company's assumptions, shaping its behavior, dictating "...its decisions about what to do and what not to do" (Drucker 1994), who to consider being customers and competitors, which technology to use and even what are considered the organization's strengths and weaknesses.

Nonaka (1991) mentions the "conceptual umbrella" identifying the common features linking activities and businesses into a coherent whole.

Table 1 provides an overview of phrases used to describe mental models.

In general, a business' purpose, its overall vision and mission, or strategic intent can also be considered determining factors of a company's mental model and thus its business definition.

• Managerial perceptions	• Mindscapes
• Blinkered perceptions	• Worldview
• Cognitive maps	• Sacred cows
• Interpretive schemes	• Managerial lenses
• Implicit theories	• Assumptions
• Screens	• Mental pictures
• Frames	• Organizing frameworks
• Templates	• Strategic frames
• Causal maps	• Construed reality
• Core causal beliefs	• Shared perspectives
• Industry recipes	• Dominant logic
• Perception filters	• Blind spots
• Belief structures	• Organizational schema
• Strategic myopia	• Tunnel vision
• Tacit understanding	• Organizational ideologies

Table 1 - Another Way of Saying "Mental Model" (Markides 2000)

As we have seen in companies usually do not question these mental models and the businesses they are in, because they focus too much on imitating their competitors. They take the industry rules and norms as a given and do not challenge these.

But redefining the business by challenging conventional wisdom and industry assumptions, and thus shifting a company's strategic focus and ultimately leaving the strategy frontier of best practices, is a first step to break free from the herd and differentiate the company from industry peers (Markides 1997; Kim and Mauborgne 1999; Yates and Skarzynski 1999; Markides 2000). And as Drucker (2002) notes, a simple change in perception can open up big innovation opportunities, an argument supported by Mintzberg (1994) saying that real strategic change requires inventing new categories (the term he uses for "mental models"), i.e. new levels of strategy, new products, new business units, etc. Senge (1996) adds that learning and change can only take place once one looks inside, identifies her mental models, and starts questioning these.

Levitt (2004) raised the question "What business are you really in?" already in his landmark 1960 article "Marketing Myopia", in which he explained that major industry leaders had come into trouble because they defined their business from a product perspective rather than from a customer perspective. The railroads for example saw themselves in the railway business instead of being in the transportation business. They were railroad (i.e. product) oriented instead of being transportation (i.e. customer) oriented. Ohmae (1982) shares Levitt's view by saying that the "business domain" should always be stated in the users' objectives.

Considering their thoughts we can argue that there are two traditional ways of defining a business:

(1) by the product sold (e.g. MP3 players), or

(2) by the customer function fulfilled (e.g. experience music wherever one is).

Hamel and Prahalad (1990; 1997) brought forward a third possibility:

(3) by the underlying core competencies of the company (e.g. design and usability capabilities).

The product-centric and core competencies views can be regrouped as being inside-out perspectives, trying to align internal strengths with the external environment, while the customer-centric view portrays an outside-in perspective, taking the environment as a starting point.

De Wit and Meyer go a step further by defining a business as "...a set of related product-market combinations" (De Wit and Meyer 2004), meaning a business lies at the intersection of what the customers or a market wants from the demand side and what a particular industry offers at the supply side. An industry can generally be defined as a group of companies offering a similar type of product or service, whereas a market is a group of customers with similar needs[2] (Figure 4).

---

[2] For a more thorough discussion on the difference between „industry" and „market" see Nightingale, John, „On the definition of Industry and Market" The Journal of Industrial Economics, Vol. 28 No. 1 September 1978

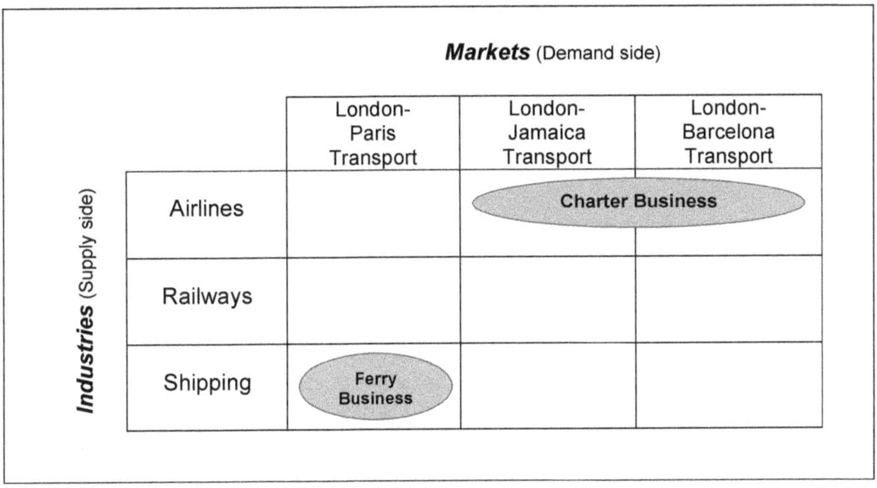

		London-Paris Transport	London-Jamaica Transport	London-Barcelona Transport
Industries (Supply side)	Airlines		Charter Business	
	Railways			
	Shipping	Ferry Business		

Markets (Demand side)

Figure 4 - Industries, Markets and Businesses (De Wit and Meyer 2004)

Abell (1980) suggests that there might be a serious danger in defining a business in product-market terms only, because the business definition might be seen as a choice of products on the one hand and markets on the other and suggests the three dimensions – costumer groups, customer function, and technology – seen above, his argument being that products are usually defined in terms of their technology and the customer functions they perform.

As noted earlier an element of strategy is its focus. The act of focusing within an industry on a particular market need is called positioning. Finding such new and unoccupied positions is seen as a major element of strategic innovation leading to differentiation and competitive advantage (e.g. Markides 2000; Kim and Mauborgne 2005).

While there might be many ways to define a business, Abell (1980) and Markides (1997; 2000) note that there is no best way to clearly define the boundaries of a business, and no view will fit every company. The importance lies in addressing the question from different angles in order to discover what suits a particular company best. Often strategic innovation will happen the moment the traditional perspective (e.g. product-centric) is traded for a new one (e.g. competency-centric) or is expanded (Markides 2000).

Hamel (1998) argues that new opportunities emerge when companies escape a product or service centric definition of their business and see it in terms of its core competencies.

Before going into detail by answering the three questions – who is the customer, what products and services to offer, and how to do this – defining a business and its strategy, managers should start by shifting their company's strategic focus and mind set from beating competition to making it irrelevant by challenging industry assumptions and established assets and capabilities.

Challenging Industry Assumptions

"Playing by the industry leader's rules is competitive suicide."

(Gary Hamel)

According to conventional logic industry conditions are a given. They can be analyzed using Porter's five forces for example, and the industry's success, along with the success of the companies within the industry, is determined by these conditions. The purpose of challenging these conditions is to shape them actively.

As described above the strategic focus of most companies lies on benchmarking with and beating their rivals, which leads to focusing on operational effectiveness rather than the aspired success through differentiation. They compare their strengths and weaknesses with those of their competitors and monitor competitors' moves in order to build advantages and beat competitors through incremental improvements.

Strategic innovators on the other hand are not interested in whether they are better than their competitors and do not follow these. They do not react on rivals moves, but "…free up resources to identify and deliver completely new sources of value" (Kim and Mauborgne 1997).

The first step towards redefining a business is by switching this strategic focus, and thereby a company's goal, from beating the competition to achieving differentiation. This switch will enable the company to see where it can be different, instead of focusing on being better by questioning industry assumptions and fundamental beliefs (Hamel 1996; Hamel and Prahalad 1997; Kim and Mauborgne 1997; Yates and Skarzynski 1999; Koch 2000; Markides 2000; Hamel 2002; Kim and Mauborgne 2004; Kim and Mauborgne 2005).

In order to challenge industry boundaries managers can look across substitute industries (Kim and Mauborgne 1997; Kim and Mauborgne 1999; Kim and Mauborgne 1999; Koch 2000; Kim and Mauborgne 2004; Kim and Mauborgne 2005) and ask what makes customers trade between different industries. "In the broadest sense, a company competes not only with the other firms in its industry but also with companies in those industries that produce alternative products or services. Alternatives include products and services that have different functions and forms but the same purpose" (Kim and Mauborgne 2005), as compared to substitutes which have the same functions and forms.

Every choice customers make is associated with certain trade-offs between possible solutions to a problem. Having some spare time one can chose to watch TV, read a book, have a coffee, or go to the fitness club. Companies can ask themselves why customers prefer a particular product or service. What makes customers trade between two different products or services? Is it price, cost, convenience, design, functionality, which functionalities in particular, or rather an emotional appeal? Considering the introductory quote about Starbucks not being in the coffee business we clearly see the point.

Another possibility is to stay within the industry but look across strategic groups. A strategic group is usually defined as a group of companies in an industry pursuing a similar strategy (Kim and Mauborgne 1999; Kim and Mauborgne 2005). Asking what makes customers trade between these groups can help finding a new business definition.

Koch (2000), Förster and Kreuz (2005), as well as Yates and Skarzynski (1999) suggest companies should not only look across strategic groups and industries, but also at other segments and countries or completely different industries and copy trends happening there, which haven't been applied to the company's industry.

Once differences and key factors have been identified the key lies in recombining these with your existing definition.

Additionally industry assumptions can be challenged by listing all the explicit beliefs in the industry and asking what would happen if one started anew.

Drucker (2002) puts forward that sometimes it is not necessary to change industry assumptions but just take advantage of major structural changes in the industry itself, which according to him happen usually when an industry grows at around 40% in ten years or less.

Choi and Välikangas (2001) argue that strategic innovators not only change the value-added structure within industries but also blur the boundaries between industries by converging value propositions, technologies and markets. They see a danger in defining the business too narrowly.

Challenging Assets & Capabilities

"Drive thy business; let it not drive thee."

(Benjamin Franklin)

Challenging assets and capabilities is part of challenging the conventional logic of a company's business. Usually management tries to leverage existing assets and capabilities, by asking "Considering what we have, what is the best we can do?" (Kim and Mauborgne 1997).

Kim and Mauborgne (1997), as well as Koch (2000) and Peters (1998) suggest that companies should not let themselves be restrained by what they have, but ask what assets and capabilities they need or would build if they started anew. Abell (1980) supports this argument by saying that a redefinition of the business can lead to a change in resource requirements, while Yates and Skarzynski (1999) argue that it is absolutely necessary to build new capabilities in the form of new forms of leadership, team work, creativity, core competencies, entrepreneurship, rapid prototyping and new venture financing to enable innovation.

Hamel (2001), Hamel and Prahalad (1989; 1997), as well as Markides (2000) and Geroski (1998) favor the opposite approach by advocating companies should look at the strengths, core competencies, strategic assets and core processes they have and ask how these can be exploited in new and creative ways, the aim being to create an unfamiliar fit between what a company has, and what it tries to accomplish with these assets. Their idea is not so much about challenging the assets and capabilities the company owns, but challenging the way they are being utilized.

It might be questionable how the reinvention of markets and complete industries, a goal always cited in connection with strategic innovation (Markides 1997; Hamel 1998; Hamel 1998; Markides 2000; Hamel 2001; e.g. Christensen and Raynor 2003; Kim and Mauborgne 2005), can be achieved when only existing resources, competencies, assets and capabilities are put to use. On the other hand it seems very unlikely that a company can afford to throw everything over board and start completely from scratch.

Collis and Montgomery (1995) add to the discussion that resources cannot be evaluated in isolation, because their value is determined in interplay with market forces. The company's internal capabilities, what it does well, need to be aligned with its external industry environment, what the market demands and what competitors offer.

It seems worth noting that Hamel and Prahalad's (1989; 1990), who originally coined the notion of core competencies, idea was to leverage existing resources by using them in new ways to create growth, while focusing on core competencies to diversify instead of focusing on businesses.

Today the concept has rather become synonymous with "focus" on those activities a company does best, i.e. it does not diversify. Whereas the first view opens up new opportunities, the second one closes such opportunities out. The first approach seems to be in line with the idea of strategic innovation, if the capabilities are used in new and creative ways that enable the creation of increased value. Interestingly Hamel himself (2001) later uses core competencies in the context of focus.

Markides also reminds us of the danger, which rests with the second approach: "it is inward looking" (Markides 2000) and asks what happens if the competencies one has are not the ones required by the market or what if the competitive situation in the industry changes?

As mentioned before the key to strategic innovation might rest in simply assessing which view the company has employed in the past and switching to the opposite approach.

Although existing assets and capabilities might not be abandoned easily, they need to be challenged on a regular basis.

Slywotzky and Wise (2003) put forward a third possibility, namely learning to mobilize hidden assets. They suggest looking beyond the traditional financial view on assets in order to find intangible assets like "...unique customer access, technical know-how, an installed base of equipment, a window on the market, a network of relationships, by-product information, or a loyal user community" (Slywotzky and Wise 2003).

Kaplan and Norton (2004) consider "measuring the value of such intangible assets [as] the holy grail of accounting" and offer the categorization – human capital, information capital, and organization capital – helping to assess the strategic readiness of intangible assets.

Christensen and Overdorf (2000) support this argument by saying that when it comes to assessing a company's capabilities, not only resources, be they tangible or intangible, are worth looking at, but also the processes, formal and informal, visible and less visible, as well as the values of a company are important capabilities to consider. Koch (2000) adds that skills of employees need also to be taken into account. How effective are the employees at doing what the customer wants?

According to De Wit and Meyer, no generally accepted classification of firm resources has yet emerged, but they present common distinctions (Figure 5).

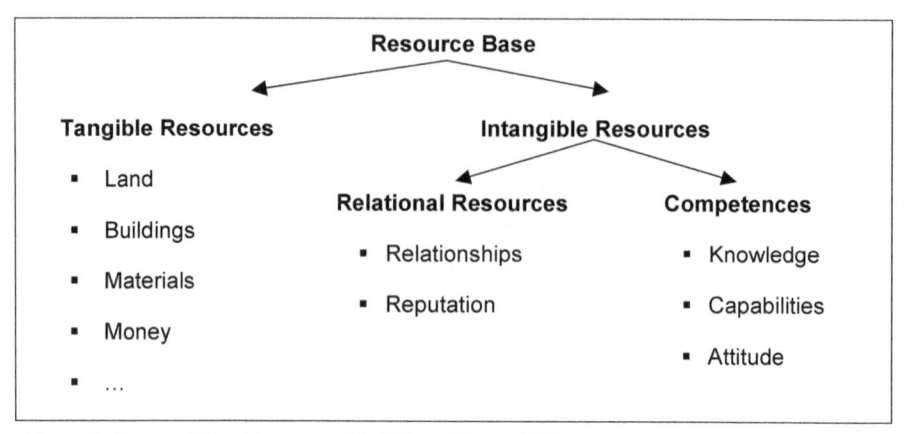

```
                        Resource Base
                       ←             →
   Tangible Resources              Intangible Resources
                                    ←             →
     • Land              Relational Resources    Competences
     • Buildings
                           • Relationships         • Knowledge
     • Materials
                           • Reputation            • Capabilities
     • Money
                                                   • Attitude
     • ...
```

Figure 5 - Types of Firm Resources (De Wit and Meyer 2004)

Think also about how you would set up the industry or the business from scratch. "You are not allowed to use the existing systems in answering this question." (Koch 2000)

Ohmae (1982) also suggests to challenge the constraints, arguing if one starts by thinking of all the things that cannot be done, and asking what possibilities are left, one will be unable to break out of the existing situation.

The following three chapters will go into more detail on how to define the business a company is in and will help to determine which assets and capabilities are needed and offer further questions and triggers to challenge the existing view.

The essential questions to ask when it comes to redefining the business are:

- What are the main industry assumptions, when it comes to pricing, costumers, products and services offered, delivery, etc.?
- Does the industry have a product-centric, customer-centric, or rather competency-centric approach? What would a change in approach entail?
- Do you let yourself be constrained by the assets and capabilities you possess?
- Are you trying to use the assets you have and simply leverage them, or are you continuously striving to build new assets?
- How many of your competitors do already posses the same or similar assets?

- Which of your assets are truly unique and cannot be imitated or substituted easily by others?
- Do companies without these assets face a cost disadvantage in obtaining them?
- Which of your assets and capabilities are obsolete?
- Which assets would you build if you started anew?
- Ask "What if...?"

Redefining the market

"Put simply, the right way to define a good customer is to pick a definition that suits you better than it does your competitors."

(Markides 2000 58)

We have identified new markets, by either creating new ones or reshaping existing ones, earlier as one of the possible outcomes of strategic innovation. Redefining the market either means (1) identifying new customer groups or (2) reshaping existing markets, which usually also leads to new segments and thus new customer groups. As no clean boundaries can be drawn between the two approaches, they will be discussed simultaneously.

Kim and Mauborgne (1999; 2005) put forward the idea of looking across the chain of buyers, instead of focusing just on one specific link in the buying process. Frequently the user of a product or service is not the buyer, and the buying decision might be influenced by a third party. Often these three roles do overlap; often they differ. In such a case, it is worth looking at what the different roles appreciate most in a purchasing decision and how they define value. For the buyer cost might be the most important factor, while the user values the ease of use, and the influencer might be keen on functionality or ease of maintenance. Discovery of a new customer group can happen if one looks at the chain of buyers and targets a different group than the one the company and the industry is currently focusing on. Maybe the company's existing cost base or skills are more valued by another group than the present target customers (Koch 2000). For a training company offering business administration and finance seminars for example, the chief financial officer might be a better target than human resources.

Hammer (2001) suggests looking beyond the distribution chains of wholesalers, distributors, retailers, dealers and all other intermediaries to focus on the final customer.

Many authors (Hamel and Prahalad 1997; Kim and Mauborgne 1997; Kim and Mauborgne 1999; Koch 2000; Markides 2000; Christensen, Johnson et al. 2002; Pearson 2002; Christensen and Raynor 2003; Kim and Mauborgne 2005) suggest looking at noncustomers as a potential new market and turn these noncustomers into new demand. Christensen and Bower (1995) even suggest that companies fail because they stay close to their existing customer base.

Kim and Mauborgne (2005) identified three tiers of noncustomers (Figure 6). The first tier consists of what they call "soon-to-be" noncustomers, who minimally use the current offering, but are constantly searching for something better and ready to switch easily. They are closest to the existing customers.

The second tier are the "refusing" noncustomers, "...people who either do not use or cannot afford to use the current market offerings because they find the offerings unacceptable or beyond their means" (Kim and Mauborgne 2005) or too complicated (Christensen and Raynor 2003) to use. The key here is that these customers are willing to buy, but not at the current terms.

The third tier of "unexplored" noncustomers is the farthest away from the existing market. Typically they are being ignored completely as potential customers by the industry, either because they have always been assumed to belong to another industry or are not being considered worth the effort.

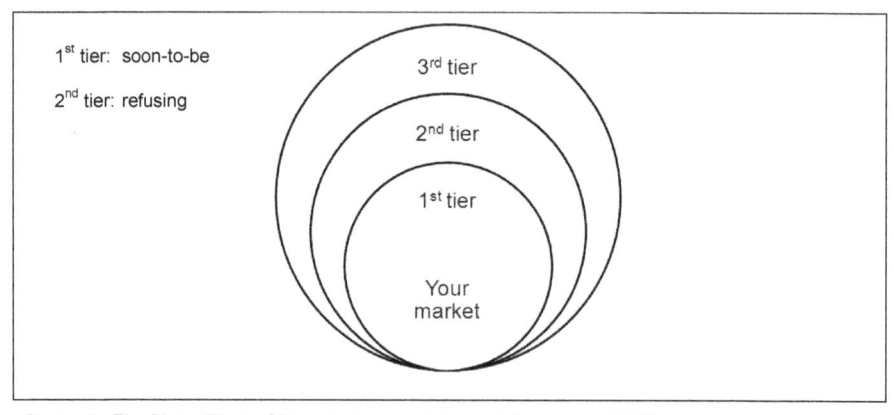

Figure 6 - The Three Tiers of Noncustomers (Kim and Mauborgne 2005)

Hamel (1996) supports the argument that looking at the total imaginable market might offer great potential for creating new demand, a strategy called "universalization" by Choi and

Välikangas (2001): going from an elite market to the masses. Examples of companies who did this include JP Morgan, Southwest Airlines, Ralph Lauren, and Karl Lagerfeld.

Markides (1997; 2000) also supports the argument to look at existing segments and think about whether there are certain segments that are not being served by the industry at the moment and target these with specific offerings.

Despite conventional logic suggesting to pick the market segment with the most satisfied or most profitable customers (Porter 1996), Christensen et al. (Christensen and Bower 1995; Christensen, Johnson et al. 2002; Christensen and Raynor 2003) put forward the idea of looking at less profitable customers as a way of tapping into unmet demand with new product offerings or with the existing cost base and skills as seen above.

Conventional logic also suggests staying close to the existing customers and to invest in technologies and offerings necessary to retain these, instead of looking at noncustomers or future customers and their demands (Christensen 1997; Christensen, Johnson et al. 2002). Christensen et al. (Christensen, Johnson et al. 2002) also point out that it is much easier to target potential customers who are not buying at all than to steal customers from competitors.

While for Kim and Mauborgne (1997; 1999; 2005) it is fundamental to find commonalities among groups (desegmentation) and target the mass of noncustomers with shared needs, instead of focusing on differences, other authors (Hamel 1996; Choi and Välikangas 2001; Prahalad and Ramaswamy 2004) recommend to focus on the individual customer and her very special, individual desires (finer segmentation, mass-customization), the argument being that customers want to be unique. Zook (2004) also mentions that finer segmentation can uncover major new growth opportunities.

Either or, as seen earlier "strategic innovation happens when you can switch your thinking from one line of thought to the other" (Markides 2000) and challenge the established industry logic.

While looking across the chain of buyers or the three tiers of noncustomers it is essential to ask why these people are not taking advantage of the current offerings to gain new insights.

Whereas new markets and customers might offer the most potential, Markides' (2000) first priority is to evaluate the existing customer base.

According to Markides (2000) the reason for thinking about existing markets and customer segments "...is to re-segment the established customer base in a creative way, so as to discover new segments that no one else has thought of" (Markides 2000).

Markets can be segmented using many different criteria, the most common being by product, price, geography, demographics, social factors, psychographics, etc[3].

While Pearson (2002) notes that demographics rarely produce meaningful segments, Drucker (2002) writes of changes in demographics being a very reliable sources of innovation opportunities. Markides (2000) also argues that new customer needs, which can stem from changes in demographics, bear tremendous potential.

Hamel (1996) as well as Förster and Kreuz (2005) suggest working against the traditional geographical orientation of the industry, by focusing on the local or regional market instead of going global, or vice versa. Markides (2000) adds that the choice of the geographic region is the first decision a company needs to take when it comes to identifying possible customers, while Zook (2004) argues that expanding into new geographic areas is consistently underestimated in complexity and bears lower than average success rates.

As seen above Kim and Mauborgne (1997; 1999; 2005) favor segmentation along commonalities in consumer needs, instead of focusing on the differences as suggested by Hamel (1996), criteria that can equally well be applied to the existing customer base.

Christensen et al. (Christensen and Raynor 2003; Christensen, Raynor et al. 2003) argue that markets are usually segmented "...along the lines for which data are available, rather than in ways that reflect the things that customers are trying to get done" (Christensen and Raynor 2003). The critical unit of analysis should be the circumstances in which customers buy or use products and services and not attributes of customers or the product itself (Christensen and Raynor 2003).

Markides (2000) and Hamel (1996; 2001) also recommend thinking beyond the products and services the company sells, identify the underlying functionality of the product and ask what need it fulfils and then try to think of possible segments with similar needs not being served at present.

---

[3] The issue of segmentation is covered thoroughly in most marketing texts, e.g. Philip Kotler (2005) "Marketing Management", Prentice Hall or Warren J. Keegan, Schlegelmilch B. (2000) "Global Marketing Management: A European Perspective", Prentice Hall International

Hammer (2001) supports the argument that customers are not interested in companies or products and services but that they only care about how their problem is being solved.

Markides (2000), as well as Slywotzky and Wise (2003) argue that, although one might look at the customer and ask what they are trying to get done, it might also be a good starting point to ask first what particular needs a product satisfies and then figuring what other customer segments with the same needs could be targeted, and thus creating a new, possibly larger segment.

As we have already seen, some authors (Hamel and Prahalad 1989; Markides 2000; Hamel 2001) favor this approach of asking how existing, unique assets, capabilities and competencies can be leveraged and used to do more for selected customers, while others (Kim and Mauborgne 1997; Kim and Mauborgne 1999; Christensen and Raynor 2003; Kim and Mauborgne 2005) dismiss this view as being conventional logic.

Geroski (1998) combines the two views by arguing that it is necessary to ask why a product is bought, i.e. what need the buyer or user tries to fulfill, or to speak in Christensen's words, "what job has to be done", and having identified the function, it is also necessary to ask how the need is satisfied.

Instead of finding a way of satisfying a particular customer need, the former suggest finding a particular customer segment in need of the particular product a company is offering.

Markides (2000) argues that benefits from core competencies and diversification can be put to use to improve a firm's operations in a new product market and to create new capabilities in a new market faster or at a lower cost than competitors could do, and thus avoid costly mistakes when entering new markets.

According to Geroski (1998) by matching unique internal resources with outside opportunities a company creates a distinct market. Another company with different competencies will always be serving a somewhat different market, although they might overlap. He further argues that even though companies "...may give similar answers to the 'who?' question, they answer the 'what?' or 'why?' and 'how?' questions quite differently" (Geroski 1998).

Once all the possible segments have been identified the question remains of which ones to target. As we have seen above different approaches are imaginable. Below is a list of things to consider:

- Who are currently your costumers?
- What are their needs?
- Why are they buying your product? What jobs are customers trying to get done?
- Which customer needs is your product actually fulfilling?
- Are there customers you are not serving now who have similar needs?
- Which customer needs and functions can be satisfied best with the company's unique competencies?
- Which customers value most what the company does best?
- Are there any existing customer segments being neglected by the industry now? Why are they not being served?
- Which consumers or customer groups share the most commonalities?
- Are competitors serving segments your company is not? Why?
- Is your company serving markets that competitors are not serving? Why?
- Who is the real final customer?
- How can existing assets and capabilities be leveraged?

Table 2 summarizes the decisions and tensions involved with identifying new customers.

existing	⇔	noncustomers (2nd and 3rd tier)
most profitable	⇔	less profitable
most satisfied	⇔	less satisfied (1st tier)
specific buyer	⇔	chain of buyers
focus on differences	⇔	focus on commonalities
focus on finer segmentation	⇔	focus on desegmentation
focus on attributes (of customers and products)	⇔	focus on circumstances (needs and the job done)

Table 2 - Redefining the Market: Which Customers to Target?

Redefining the product

"...ferret out what customers really want (instead of what they say they want)."

Andrall E. Pearson (2002)

Asking what products or services to offer customers is another strategic question companies must ask themselves. Just as they cannot target everyone as their customer, they also have to focus their offerings (Markides 2000).

Although Abell (1980) notes that the product is only the outcome of the decisions of how (i.e. which technology to use) to satisfy a particular need, and other authors argue that a product-centric view can be dangerous as we have seen above, most of them also identify changes in the product or services offered, or the introduction of new offerings, as enablers of strategic innovation leading to new markets, new demand and value improvements for the customer and the company (Geroski 1998; Markides 2000; Kim and Mauborgne 2005).

According to Zook "Selling a new product or new services to core customers is one of the most commonly pursued and highest-potential [strategies]" (Zook 2004).

How can opportunities for new offerings be identified?

As we have seen above, looking at the customer is a first step. As described earlier the traditional tools for market research have their limits, the most important being that customers can only tell us about their perceived needs. "Determining what the company has to do to meet them requires making an admittedly difficult creative leap." (Markides 2000) Furthermore consumers have been conditioned in what to expect by a lot of industries: "more of the same for less" (Kim and Mauborgne 1999), and will probably not think creatively about new offerings.

Both arguments are supported by Nordström and Ridderstråle (2002) who reason that most products we enjoy today, we would not have wanted if they had been offered to us at the start of their development. They furthermore argue that if companies want to invent something really interesting and revolutionary, they need to learn to ignore customers, the argument being that most of them are extremely conservative and lack the necessary imagination.

Nevertheless, the customer can be an important source for new product ideas.

Toolkits for user innovation for example are an alternative approach to simple market research "...in which manufacturers actually abandon the attempt to understand user needs in detail in favor of transferring need-related aspects of product and service development to users" (Hippel and Katz 2002). "Toolkits for user innovation are coordinated sets of 'user-friendly' design tools that enable users to develop new product innovations for themselves. The toolkits are not general purpose. Rather, they are specific to the design challenges of a specific field or subfield, such as integrated circuit design or software product design. Within their fields of use, they give users real freedom to innovate, allowing them to develop producible custom products via iterative trial and error. That is, users can create a preliminary design, simulate or prototype it, evaluate its functioning in their own use environment, and then iteratively improve it until satisfied." (Hippel and Katz 2002)

Hippel and Katz (2002) point out that such toolkits are most valuable in highly heterogeneous markets. Thomke and Hippel (2002) add that toolkits make most sense, when (1) market segments are shrinking and customers are increasingly asking for customized products, which increases costs that are difficult to pass on to customers, (2) the producer as well as customers need many iterations before a solution is found, which results in erosion of customer loyalty, and finally (3), when the company uses high-quality computer-based simulation and rapid-prototyping tools internally.

Such integration of the customer into the whole experience of designing the product might also lead to improved customer relationships and higher retention.

Prahalad and Ramaswamy go even as far as to say that "A firm cannot create anything of value without the engagement of individuals" (Prahalad and Ramaswamy 2004) and put forward the idea of individual centered co-creation of value by actively engaging in an open dialogue with customers, offering interaction experiences and by providing transparent access to all sorts of company information to them (Prahalad and Ramaswamy 2004; Prahalad and Ramaswamy 2004).

Zook (2004) supports the argument giving examples of companies the best growth ideas for new products of which came from customers. Brown (2002) also suggests the customer being the research department's ultimate innovation partner.

Instead of asking the customers directly one might also try finding out more about what it is they are trying to get done, by observing them (Kawasaki 2000; Kelley 2001; Drucker 2002; Pearson 2002; Christensen and Raynor 2003), or seeking feedback from, distributors, the customers' customers, competitors, employees, suppliers, peers, etc. and try to understand the value chain they are all imbedded in (Markides 2000).

Putting oneself in the shoes of a customer is often claimed being among the best ways to identify pain points, either in regard to the function customers are trying to fulfill, or the use of the product (Kawasaki 2000; Koch 2000; Kelley 2001). Trying out different products, substitutes, and alternatives also enables one to identify the advantages and disadvantages of available alternatives.

Instead of relying on market research carried out by an external institute or reports from employees, managers are also advised to go out themselves and talk to the customer directly (Hamel and Välikangas 2003).

As seen above many researchers (Abell 1980; Hamel 1996; Geroski 1998; Markides 2000; Christensen and Raynor 2003; Christensen, Raynor et al. 2003) suggest understanding what customers are trying to do when buying a product and what alternatives they use for fulfilling the same function. What are the functions of the product? Why are they buying or using it? Asking or observing consumers with focus on these questions might lead to new ways of performing the job.

Furthermore while looking at the chain of buyers or the three tiers of noncustomers or resegmenting the existing market it is essential to ask why these people are not satisfied or not taking advantage of the current offerings to gain possible insights for new products and services. The product might be too complex or too expensive, as it is often the case for second tier customers.

Simplifying product offerings can be used to have a clear and precise offering (Förster and Kreuz 2005). Where might less be better? As Christensen (1997) has shown disruptive innovation happens when a lower end product is offered to a niche which then becomes the mass market. In this case the product must be "...targeted at customers who will be happy with a simple product" (Christensen, Johnson et al. 2002).

According to Christensen et al. (Christensen, Johnson et al. 2002) a key to seeing whether consumers have been over served is to look at whether they are willing to pay premium prices for further improvements of a product or service. If so, consumers are not yet over served and the market or consumer group cannot be disrupted.

While Koch (2000) suggests to build in extra features, services, and quality, Kim and Mauborgne (1997; 1999; 2005) propose the following four questions for identifying and changing key elements of the product, the service and delivery, as the three platforms on which innovation can take place:

(1) What factors should be *reduced* well below the industry standard?

(2) What factors should be *raised* well beyond the industry standard?

(3) What factors should be *created* that the industry never offered?

(4) What factors should be *eliminated* that the industry has taken for granted?

As seen above, while looking at customers and noncustomers companies can look across alternative industries or strategic groups within their industry to assess why people are buying substitutes from other industries or trading up or down between strategic groups. Determine how customers make trade-offs across substitutes, capture the rewards of trading up or down and offer the decisive advantages of both offerings. (Kim and Mauborgne 1999; Kim and Mauborgne 2005)

Pearson (2002) Koch (2000), Markides (2000), as well as Choi and Välikangas (2001) support this approach and put forward that good ideas can come from various outside sources: products and services offered by companies in similar industries, outside industries, or in other countries, from conventional competitors, regionals, small companies, competitors on other continents, and so on. Pearson adds that to him "...it amounts to finding out what's working with consumers, improving on the concept, and getting more out of it" (Pearson 2002). Stalk and Lachenauer even proclaim to "plagiarize with pride" (Stalk and Lachenauer 2004).

Instead of adding new features or reshaping existing products, organizations can also think of launching complementary products and services. In most cases products are not used on their own in a vacuum but their value is affected by other products and services. Think of a total solution buyers seek and solve consumers' problems focusing on the major pain points or even along the entire value chain. What happens, before, during and after the company's product is used? (Kim and Mauborgne 1997; Peters 1998; Kim and Mauborgne 1999; Choi and Välikangas 2001; Govindarajan and Gupta 2001; Hamel 2001; Hammer 2001; Kim and Mauborgne 2005; Sawhney, Wolcott et al. 2006) Examples of companies having done this include Cineplexx movie theatres, Starbucks, Barnes & Noble, most out of town shopping centers, and many hotels offering for example kids day care and wellness facilities.

Roussel and Nunes (2003) argue that bundling products and services into combinations, will persuaded consumers to pay a premium and remain highly loyal.

Kim and Mauborgne (1999; 2005) also point out that competition in a certain industry usually converges around either a functional or an emotional appeal of the product. Innovation is possible by shifting that focus.

An argument supported by other researchers who add that companies should be offering experiences and not only products or services (Choi and Välikangas 2001; Hamel 2001; Peters 2003; Prahalad and Ramaswamy 2003; Prahalad and Ramaswamy 2004; Prahalad and Ramaswamy 2004; Sawhney, Wolcott et al. 2006). Examples of companies having achieved this include Apple, Starbucks, Swatch, or the Body Shop.

Lindner and Cantrell (2000) suggest that the usual evolution is to shift from products to services and from services to experiences. They also put forward the idea of either bundling or unbundling offerings.

Design is also being considered a vital ingredient to a product's emotional appeal and new product innovation in general (Peters 1998; Kelley 2001; Nordström and Ridderstråle 2002; Peters 2003; Godin 2004; Förster and Kreuz 2005).

Another way of identifying new product opportunities is by looking at emerging trends in and outside the industry (Kim and Mauborgne 1999; Yates and Skarzynski 1999; Markides 2000; Kim and Mauborgne 2005) and changing customer priorities (Markides 1997). Kim and Mauborgne point out that innovation rarely arises from projecting the trend itself, but rather from "…business insights into how the trend will change value to customers and impact the company's business model" (Kim and Mauborgne 2005) but they also mention that this is the most difficult approach as the trend, in order to form a basis for strategic innovation, "…must be decisive to your business, … must be irreversible, and … must have a clear trajectory" (Kim and Mauborgne 2005). Koch (2000) suggests asking what impact do technology trends and the internet have on the business and the product.

Kambil and Eselius (1999) argue that new value for the customer can also be created along the five dimensions of customer interactions: buying, using, selling/transferring, co-creating, and integrating, value always being the difference between perceived benefits and perceived costs. The relationship between cost and value can be summarized using the cost-value curve (Figure 7).

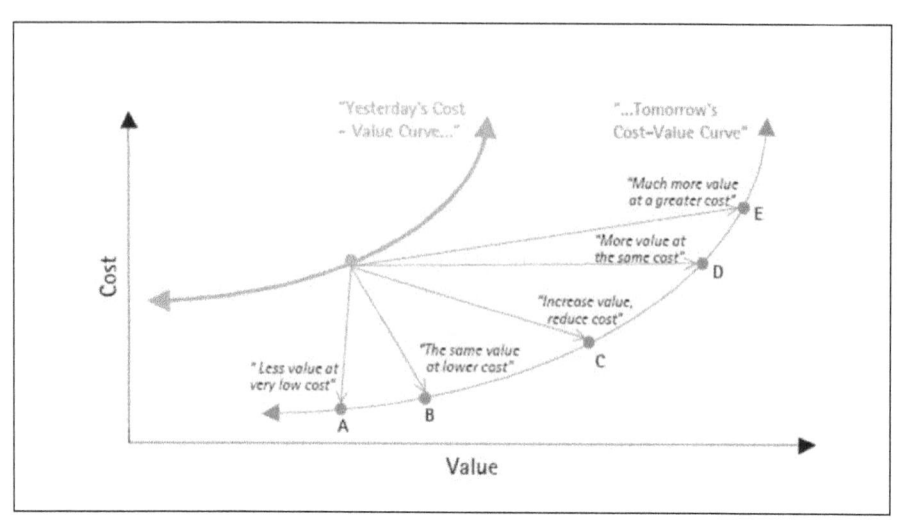

Figure 7 - Shifting the Customer Value Frontier (Kambil and Eselius 1999)

Kim and Mauborgne (2000; 2005) have identified six such stages of buyer experience – purchase, delivery, use, supplements, maintenance, and disposal – and suggest using these to assess the utility and commercial potential of new business ideas. The underlining question is "...where and how the new product or service will change the lives of its consumers" (Kim and Mauborgne 2000).

The buyer utility test can not only be used to evaluate the potential of a new product or service, but also to identify possible areas for increasing the value for consumers and nonconsumers alike, by identifying and reducing blocks to buyer utility.

Table 3 summarizes the six stages of the buyer experience cycle along with the six utility levers.

	The Six Stages of the Buyer Experience Cycle					
	Purchase	Delivery	Use	Supplements	Maintenance	Disposal
The Six Utility Levers	Customer Productivity:	In which stage are the biggest blocks to customer productivity?				
	Simplicity:	In which stage are the biggest blocks to simplicity?				
	Convenience:	In which stage are the biggest blocks to convenience?				
	Risk:	In which stage are the biggest blocks reducing risk?				
	Fun and image:	In which stage are the biggest blocks fun and image?				
	Environmental friendliness:	In which stage are the biggest blocks to environmental friendliness?				

Table 3 - Uncovering the Blocks to Buyer Utility (Kim and Mauborgne 2005)

Markides (2000) also stresses the need for evaluating ideas. Whereas the customers' wants or needs that we may have identified when thinking about the market can help us identify what the company *could* be offering, it seems essential to apply many more criteria before deciding what the company *should* be offering. The buyer utility assessment is one element to consider. Further elements include, again, existing assets and capabilities. Are they truly unique? Can they be leveraged or maybe used in a different setting or combination? (Hamel and Prahalad 1997)

To visualize the new product or service offering Kim and Mauborgne (1997; 1999; 2005) have developed the so called "value curve" or "strategy canvas", illustrating the key elements of the product, service, delivery and other factors of competition and their respective level, usually defined as being low, mid or high.

Figure 8 shows the strategy canvas for Southwest Airlines compared to the average airline and an alternative industry: car transportation. As we can see Southwest has reduced a considerable number of elements the industry had taken for granted (e.g. meals, lounges, seating class choices), while at the same time increasing others (e.g. service, speed). They also managed to dramatically reduce cost and thereby price.

Kim and Mauborgne (2005) believe that value innovation only happens when buyer value can be increased while lowering at the same time cost, and hence argue that a company must not make the value-cost trade off, but strive to achieve both.

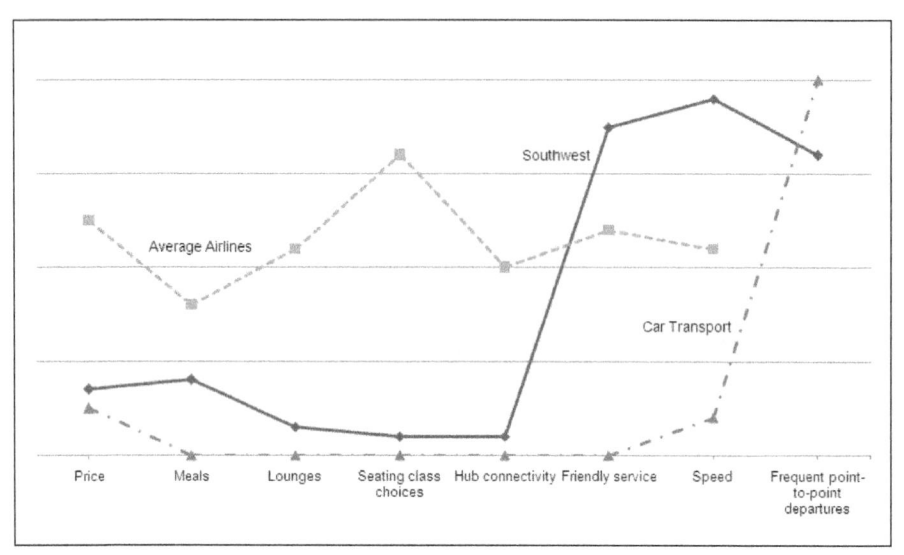

Figure 8 - The Strategy Canvas of Southwest Airlines (Kim and Mauborgne 2005)

The following list summarizes questions to consider while thinking about which products and services to offer.

- Which of your assets, capabilities, and core competencies are truly unique?
- Which of those are valued by the customer?
- What are the customers' needs and wants? What is the job they are trying to get done? What is the problem they are trying to solve?
- What job can customers not get done?
- How could you build on your core competencies to fulfill these needs better or fulfill different needs with new products?
- Why are noncustomers not using your offering?
- Which elements of your offerings could be reduced, raised, created, or eliminated so as to fulfill noncustomers' needs?
- What could a total solution, making the customers' total experience more worthwhile, look like?
- Could the customers design the products or parts of it themselves?

- Instead of traditional market research: have you observed the customer, talked to them directly, and tried the product yourself?
- What trends can be observed?
- How will they change customers' priorities?
- What offerings do alternative industries have?
- What offerings do other strategic groups have?
- What do companies in similar or even completely different industries or countries offer?
- What would less profitable customers want? How could their needs be fulfilled in a profitable way? Thus, how could they become an attractive market for your company?
- Is consumption constrained by any factors, which might be reduced?
- What do customers before, during, and after having bought your product?
- Is there anything more you could offer to make the whole experience more satisfying?
- Which emotions does your product or service evoke?
- Which alternative technologies might meet the customers' requirements? Which rivals are pursuing which approach?
- What are the two or three key parameters that influence the customers' decision to buy? How do these relate to the technical performance factors or design parameters of each alternative technology?
- How far is my company from the limits of each alternative technology? Are there ways to circumvent these limits?
- How much would the customer value the remaining technical potential? How much would it cost to realize this potential?" (Coyne, Buaron et al. 2000)
- Seek feedback and advice from external experts, suppliers, customers, and distributors.

Figure 9 summarizes spaces to consider whilst identifying new product and service offerings.

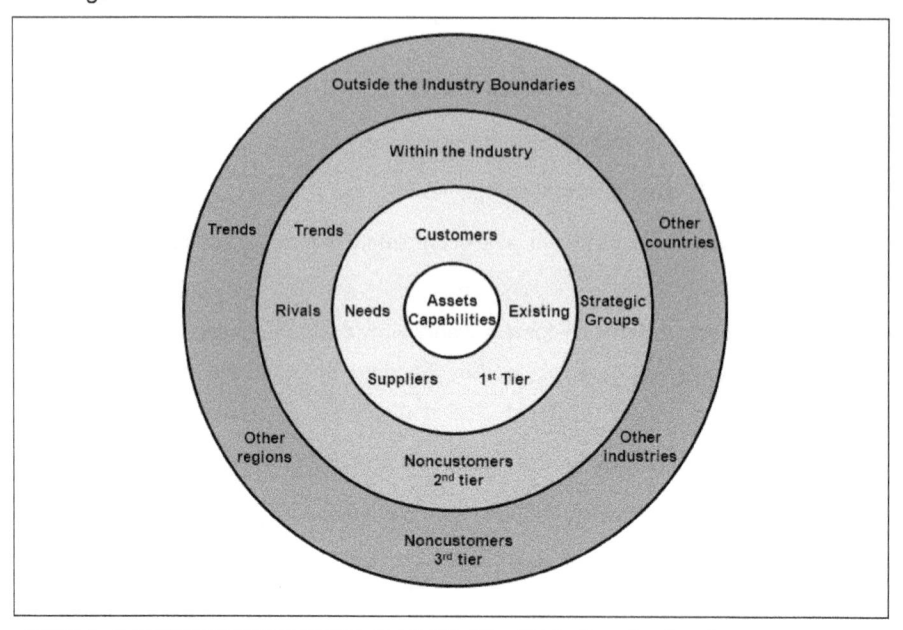

Figure 9 - Redefining the Product: How to Identify New Products or Services?

Table 4 summarizes the main decisions and tensions involved concerning the product and service offerings.

focus on existing assets	⇔	start anew, or use existing assets in a new way
single product or service	⇔	total solution, bundling
functional appeal	⇔	emotional appeal and experiences
focus on product	⇔	focus on function fulfilled and the job-to-be-done
build new features	⇔	raise, reduced, create, eliminate selectively

Table 4 - Redefining the Product: Dimensions and Tensions

Redefining the business model

As we have seen above, strategy is supposed to be a system of reinforcing activities, which have to fit both internally and externally. The following part will deal with the elements of that system.

What is a business model?

"A business model is simply the 'way of doing business' that a firm has chosen: its entire system for creating and providing consistent value to customers and earning a profit from that activity, as well as benefit for its broader stakeholders. It refers to the core architecture or configuration of the firm, specifically how it deploys all relevant resources (not just those within the company boundaries), to create differentiated value for customers at a profit..." (Davenport, Leibold et al. 2006). It is the underlying economic logic that explains how value is delivered to the customer at an appropriate cost (Magretta 2002).

The business model is a company's answer to the question of how to make money in its chosen business. It describes, "...as a system, how the pieces of a business fit together" (Magretta 2002).

Core elements of a business model

Just like with strategy in general, there seems to exist no stipulation as to what elements comprehend a business model.

According to Magretta (2002) the business model is a story telling us all about the activities associated with making something, e.g. designing, purchasing raw materials, manufacturing, and selling something, e.g. finding and reaching customers, sales, distribution.

Linder and Cantrell (2000) have identified the following elements as components of a business model (Figure 10). They illustrate furthermore how business models can be changed by illustrating the different choices a company has (Figure 11).

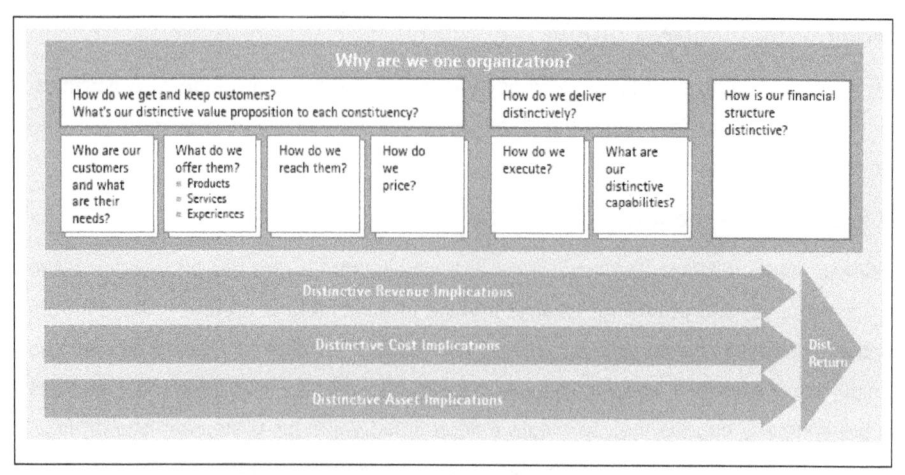

Figure 10 - Elements of a Business Model (Linder and Cantrell 2000)

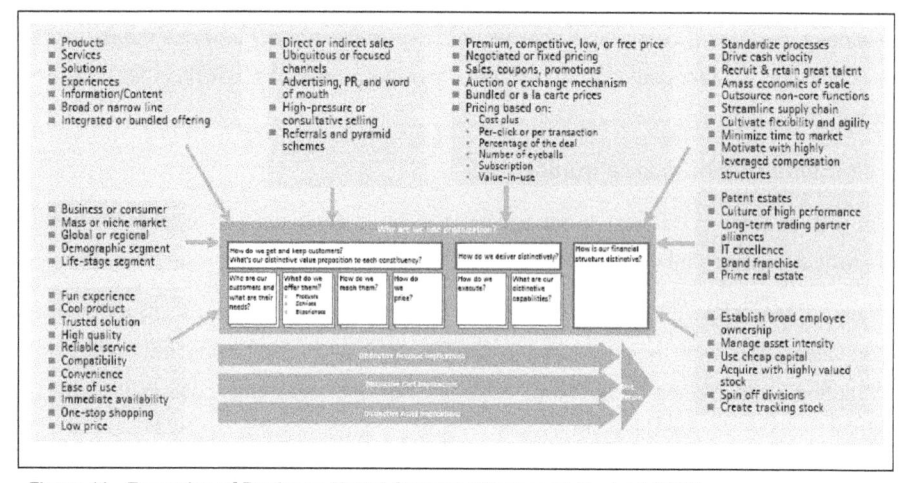

Figure 11 - Examples of Business Model Choices (Linder and Cantrell 2000)

Hamel (2001) identifies four main elements, which all have different subcomponents, and are connected through three bridging elements (Figure 12). He adds that the potential to create value is defined by four additional elements, efficiency, uniqueness, fit, and profit boosters, influencing every component of the business model and describing possible opportunities for innovation and differentiation, leading to a fundamental change in how business is conducted, an argument supported by other authors (Linder and Cantrell 2000; Magretta 2002; Davenport, Leibold et al. 2006).

Customer Benefit	*Configuration*		*Company Boundaries*
Customer Interface Fulfillment & Support Information & Insight Relationship	**Core Strategy** Business Mission Product & Market scope Differentiation	**Strategic Resources** Core Competencies Strategic Assets Core	**Value Adding Network** Suppliers Partners Alliances

Efficiency – Uniqueness – Fit – Profit Boosters

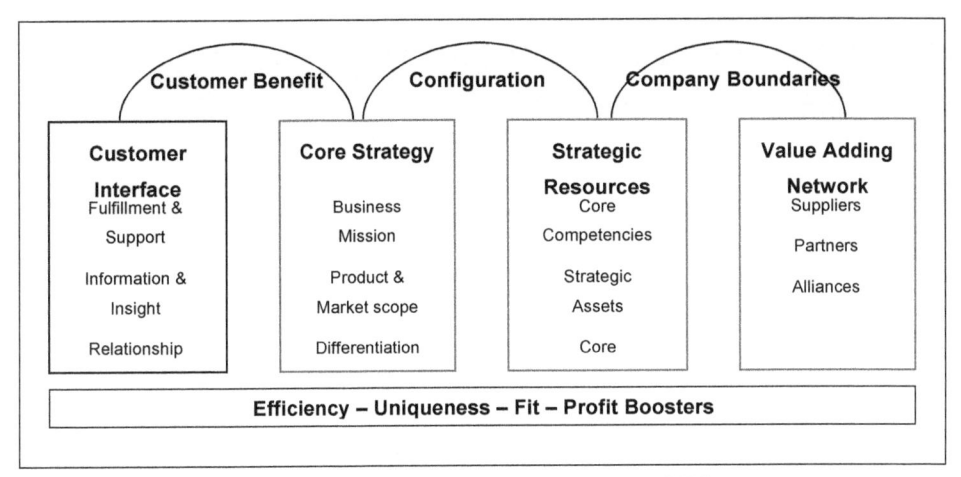

Figure 12 - Elements of Hamel's Business Model (adapted from Hamel 2001)

Drawing, among others, on Hamel's, Magretta's and Lindner and Cantrell's work, Osterwalder (2004) developed a model from the existing literature and research featuring nine business model building blocks (Table 5).

Figure 13 shows the relationships and interactions between the nine building blocks.

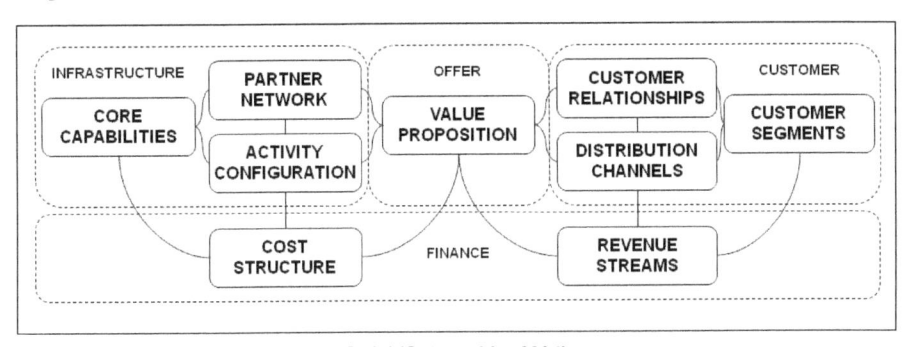

Figure 13 - Visualizing a Business Model (Osterwalder 2004)

Pillar	Building Block of Business Model	Description
Product	Value Proposition	A Value Proposition is an overall view of a company's bundle of products and services that are of value to the customer.
Customer Interface	Target Customer	The Target Customer is a segment of customers a company wants to offer value to.
	Distribution Channel	A Distribution Channel is a means of getting in touch with the customer.
	Relationship	The Relationship describes the kind of link a company establishes between itself and the customer.
Infrastructure Management	Activity Configuration	The Activity Configuration describes the arrangement of activities and resources that are necessary to create value for the customer.
	Capability	A capability is the ability to execute a repeatable pattern of actions that is necessary in order to create value for the customer.
	Partnership	A Partnership is a voluntarily initiated cooperative agreement between two or more companies in order to create value for the customer.
Financial Aspects	Cost Structure	The Cost Structure is the representation in money of all the means employed in the business model.
	Revenue Model	The Revenue Model describes the way a company makes money through a variety of revenue flows.

Table 5 - The Nine Business Model Building Blocks (Osterwalder 2004)

Essentially, having defined the value proposition and the customer, a company needs to define ways of getting to the customer. The channels for doing so can be either distribution channels for selling and delivering to the customer, but different channels can also be used for customer acquisition and retention. The offer for the customer is going to create not only revenues, but also costs to sustain the necessary infrastructure. Concerning the infrastructure the most important decisions include which activities to carry out, which of these to carry out oneself and where to outsource and collaborate with other companies.

Many definitions of business models include the customer, as well as product and service offerings as core elements. The following part will concentrate on the elements that have not been discussed above, namely:

- the customer interface, distribution channels, and relationship;
- revenue streams and pricing in particular;
- the cost structure;
- the larger network the company is embedded in, i.e. partners, suppliers, alliances;
- the configuration and fit of the activities carried out.

The customer interface, distribution channels and relationship

As seen before Prahalad and Ramaswamy suggest openly engaging with the customer to co-create value in innovative experiences. To enable this kind of interaction they suggest shifting from the traditional innovation view to what they call "experience innovation", the focus of innovation no longer being on the product and services but on co-creation experience environments. Under this view the supply chain no longer fulfils the function of delivering products and services but experience networks allowing the consumer to co-construct experiences on contextual demand (Prahalad and Ramaswamy 2003; Prahalad and Ramaswamy 2004; Prahalad and Ramaswamy 2004).

It seems clear that such a view demands a radical departure from current customer interfaces and distribution channels and that such a strategy might be best suited when strong customer relationships are essential and the market is highly heterogeneous as observed above regarding the use of toolkits for customer innovation. Prahalad and Ramaswamy (2004) mention that most companies are unable to embrace such a value co-creation strategy because it demands a radical departure from the current roles of both, the costumer and the company. They add that established companies have found it difficult to implement multichannel experience environments (Prahalad and Ramaswamy 2004) and offer the following key building blocks of co-creation summarized in their DART model:

- "*Dialogue*: Dialogue means interactivity, engagement, and a propensity to act – on both sides. Dialogue is more than listening to customers: it implies shared learning and communication between two equal problem solvers. Dialogue creates and maintains a loyal community.
- *Access*: Access begins with information and tools.
- *Risk assessment*: Risk here refers to the probability of harm to the consumer. If consumers are active co-creators, should they shoulder responsibility for risks as

well? The debate about informed consent and the responsibilities of companies and consumers will likely continue for years. However, we can safely assume that consumers will increasingly participate in co-creation of value. They will insist that businesses inform them fully about risks, providing not just data but appropriate methodologies for assessing the personal and societal risk associated with products and services.

- *Transparency*: Companies have traditionally benefited from information asymmetry between the consumer and the firm. That asymmetry is rapidly disappearing. Firms can no longer assume opaqueness of prices, costs, and profit margins. And as information about products, technologies, and business systems becomes more accessible, creating new levels of transparency becomes increasingly desirable." (Prahalad and Ramaswamy 2004)

Hamel (2001) shares the argument that companies do not only have to use the information they have about their customers but should also distribute information to customers in order to enhance the experience of buying, using and maintaining or disposing the product. Sawhney et al. also suggest redesigning "…the customer interactions across all touch points and all moments of contact" (Sawhney, Wolcott et al. 2006)

When it comes to customer interface, Hammer (2001) argues that it is necessary to have a single point of reference in charge of the total solution a customer seeks to solve her problem, offering a seamless experience across all interactions. In business-to-business markets, this could for example mean having an integrated team with an account manager, or in consumer markets having call centre agents who can actually help and solve the problem. Hammer (2001) also stresses the crucial fact of processes and customer interfaces being such that it is easy to do business with the company.

Sawhney (Sawhney, Wolcott et al. 2006) suggests thinking of new ways to reach the customer and show presence and encourage thinking creatively about fulfillment.

As we have seen above many other researchers support the argument that the company has to provide seamless experiences to customers.

While developing a channel strategy, we can use Kim and Mauborgne's six stages of buyer experience cycle – purchase, delivery, use, supplements, maintenance, and disposal – seen above to assess which channel fulfils what need in which of the six stages and make sure every stage is addressed by the channels chosen and thus a satisfying buying experience can be ensured.

Using the tool could result in a table similar to Table 6 below. Based on common marketing knowledge I added the two steps 'awareness' and 'evaluation' before the purchase decision is made. The model could be further expanded by adding possible channels, which enable interaction possibilities for co-creation as intended by Prahalad and Ramaswamy, or using other elements of the customer interface as described by Hamel or Osterwalder.

Channels	Pre-purchase steps		The Six Stages of the Buyer Experience Cycle					
	Awareness	Evaluation	Purchase	Delivery	Use	Supplements	Maintenance	Disposal
Branded stores								
Country websites								
Retailers								
All sorts of advertising								
Logistics company								

Table 6 - Assessing Distribution Channels

Of course, the channel strategy has also to be adapted to the kind of relationship and image the company wants to build with potential customers.

Kaplan and Norton (2001), building on Treacy and Wiersema's three value disciplines – operational excellence, customer intimacy and product leadership – suggest that there are three different images customers can have of a company: smart shopper, best brand, and best product. Depending on the chosen value proposition and image, companies need to establish the corresponding internal processes and distribution channels in order to be able to deliver on its chosen value proposition.

Revenue streams and pricing

The revenue model measures the ability of a company to generate money from its offerings and can consist of different revenue streams, e.g. selling, lending, licensing, transaction based cuts, advertising, etc., that can all have different pricing mechanisms (Osterwalder 2004).

Hamel (2001) puts forward the argument that what a company charges is not necessarily what a customer thinks she is paying. The company's price structure is very often different from the customer's value structure. As seen before the suggestion is to challenge conventional pricing mechanisms.

Prahalad and Ramaswamy (2004) suggest the idea of "heterogeneous pricing", prices set on experiences not on a company-centric set of product specifications or cost.

Kim and Mauborgne (2000; 2005) consider it essential to set a price that will acquire the mass of target buyers quickly and retain them. Strategic pricing is especially important when the risk of imitation is high, which is usually the case with nonrival goods, the use of which by one company does not limit the use by somebody else. In such a case the developer has to bear all the cost, the incentive is high to generate the appropriate revenue, and the accordingly large customer base early on, before the idea has been imitated. Low prices attracting the mass of buyers discourage free riding, because when having acquired the mass of the market with exceptional utility paired with a compelling ability to pay it will be difficult to convince customers to switch to another company. This fact is reinforced by network externalities saying that the value of a product or service is tied to the total number of people using it.

The fact that volume generates increasingly higher returns is reinforced by the circumstance that goods become more knowledge intensive. Development cost for the first unit might be high, whereas producing subsequent units is relatively cheap as is the case with software for example.

Thus, Kim and Mauborgne (2000; 2005) argue that if a product or service is difficult to imitate, prices can be at the upper-level, whereas vice versa they have to be low.

They also argue that, while determining the price, it is critical to price not against competitors offering the same product, but against substitutes and across alternative industries (Kim and Mauborgne 2000; Kim and Mauborgne 2005).

Other ways of pricing innovation are to go from selling a good (which might be too expensive for the mass market) to renting or leasing it, or to introduce a time-share model as with fractional ownership of private jets for example.

Osterwalder (2004) offers the following list of pricing possibilities:

- Pay-per-use
- Subscription
- List price / menu price
- Product feature dependent
- Customer characteristic dependent
- Volume dependent
- Value-based
- Bargaining
- Yield management
- Auction
- Reverse auction
- Dynamic market

Of course, for the customer the ultimate price is probably paying nothing. Förster and Kreuz (2005) suggest finding other revenue sources or payers instead of the final user of the product. LaudaMotion, a car rental business offering cars as advertising space, is such an example. Companies pay for the advertising. Rental customers pay only one Euro per day of usage.

Förster and Kreuz (2005) also put forward the idea that prices have to polarize: they either have to be high or low. Selling at the same price level as competition is unlikely to work.

The cost of doing business

Having determined the strategic price of the product that will allow companies to gain the mass of the market it is vital to establish a cost structure allowing the company to make a profit. Kim and Mauborgne argue that "price minus cost" is how strategic innovators think, as compared to the conventional logic of "cost plus" pricing. The key is "...to arrive at a cost structure that is both profitable and hard for potential followers to match" (Kim and Mauborgne 2005), a success factor often cited for Dell computers, RyanAir and other low cost carriers for example.

Kim and Mauborgne (2005) offer two levers to hit the cost target: (1) streamlining operations[4] and introducing cost innovations throughout the value chain, and (2) partnering.

While streamlining and optimizing processes it is important to remember the criticism of strategic management discussed above. The difference here is that streamlining is not a goal per se, but a means to an end, namely achieve the lowest costs possible in order to be able to offer at a price affordable by the mass market, always combined with offering superior value in the eye of the customer.

Koch (2000) suggest to consider what is the most expensive part of the existing business and find ways to decrease the cost of it.

Christensen and Raynor (2003) also point out that it is crucial to create a cost structure which allows the company to serve the customers. Especially if the company has targeted a less profitable segment as identified above.

Integrate or outsource?

Whereas Kim and Mauborgne (2005), as well as Hamel (2001) and Hammer (2001), argue that partnering "...provides a way for companies to secure capabilities fast and effectively while dropping their cost structure" (Kim and Mauborgne 2005), Christensen and Raynor (2003) question this conventional logic, which suggests if something fits a company's core competence it should be done inside, if somebody else can do it better or more cheaply, it should be outsourced.

As we have seen before the issue of assets, capabilities, and core competencies is highly controversial. Conventional logic bears the risk of "...what might seem to be a noncore activity today might become an absolute critical competence ... in the future, and vice versa" (Christensen and Raynor 2003).

According to Christensen and Raynor (2003) the answer lies with the job-to-be-done and whether the current offering is good enough to fulfill this need, or whether there is a gap between expectations and the functionality of the offering. If there is a gap they suggest a company can gain considerable competitive advantage through integration, the argument

---

[4] The issue of streamlining and process design is covered by numerous texts on Activity Based Costing, Target Costing, Six Sigma, Lean Manufacturing, Business Process Reengineering, Total Quality Management, etc.

being that integration gives the company and it engineers more flexibility to close this performance gap because, if firms must compete by making the best product they cannot simply assemble standardized components. They must be able to improve the system as a whole.

If, on the other hand the current offering has become a commodity and customers cannot see the benefits of improved functionality and are not willing to pay more for these or at least not for a particular type of improvements, companies can switch to a modular design and buy standardized components, while focusing on upgrading only certain parts of the system, namely those parts where the customer is willing to pay for improvements (Christensen and Raynor 2003).

Hamel (2001) distinguishes between suppliers, partners, and alliances. Suppliers fulfill steps in the value chain that the company has chosen to outsource, whereas partners offer additions, thus acting on a rather horizontal level as opposed to the suppliers who act on a vertical level. Alliances are coalitions with competitors. They are particular interesting if capital expenditures or risks associated with a new venture, were it developing a new technology or entering a new market, are particular high.

Hamel argues that all three players belong to the value-creating network of a company and can be used in creative ways to gain competitive advantage. He agrees with Kim and Mauborgne that certain steps may be better carried out by a company having specialized in this particular activity, but also warns against outsourcing activities that could become crucial (Hamel 2001), as recommended by Christensen and Raynor.

When it comes to working with suppliers, partners and customers, Hammer (2001) suggests companies need to knock down the barriers that hinder a transparent flow of information in order to integrate intercorporate business processes and information systems. Sawhney (Sawhney, Wolcott et al. 2006) suggests the network should be used to create integrated offerings.

Configuration and the importance of fit

After having chosen which activities to perform and which ones to outsource the question of how a reinforcing system that fits the current environment, and is still flexible enough to respond to changes in the environment, can be created remains.

The value chain, being "...the linked set of value-creating activities all the way through from basic raw material sources for component suppliers to the ultimate end-use product delivered into the final customer's hands" (Govindarajan and Gupta 2001) can be used to illustrate the interplay of the chosen activities.

As seen while defining strategic innovation, the end-to-end value chain also offers the potential for innovation.

Govindarajan and Gupta (2001) present key ideas for a value chain redesign and illustrate them with the computer manufacturer Dell.

"First, its two central attributes must be redesigned: (1) the set of activities that will constitute the new value chain and (2) the interfaces across the activities. In eliminating the role of middlemen altogether, Dell redesigned the set of activities comprising the chain. However, the company did not stop there. It built deep relationships at both ends – with suppliers as well as customers. Such virtual integration without vertical integration represents a redesign of the interface across activities on Dell's part.

Second, the new value chain must create dramatic gains in one or more of three areas: cost structure, asset investment, and speed of responsiveness to external changes. Compared to traditional competitors, Dell's direct model had the following unique combination of features: significantly lower costs, negative working capital investment, custom-built machines, first-mover advantage in offering leading-edge component technologies, high quality and reliability, an efficient and convenient purchasing process, speed of delivery, and excellent after-sales service.

Third, the new value chain must enable the company to scale up its business model to ensure rapid growth in market share, high-velocity globalization, and expansion into related products and services. On the upstream side, Dell relied totally on third-party component suppliers; on the downstream side, it completely eliminated reliance on local distributor channels; and the Net-based Dell Online channel allowed it to sell a large variety of PC-related peripheral products, such as printers and cameras. As a result, Dell's business model has perhaps been the most rapidly scalable within the PC industry." (Govindarajan and Gupta 2001)

Porter (1996) stresses the importance of fit, saying "Fit drives both competitive advantage and sustainability" (Porter 1996) and that not the individual activities determine competitive advantage, but the way activities fit together and reinforce each other. He illustrates three distinct types of fit, which are not mutually exclusive:

(1) First order fit: simple consistency between each activity (function) and the overall strategy;

(2) Second order fit, occurring when activities are reinforcing;

(3) Third order fit: optimization of effort.

Figure 14 illustrates Southwest Airlines' activity system and how the activities support and reinforce each other. The dark circles represent high-order strategic themes, which are identified and implemented through clusters of tightly linked activities (light circles).

Porter (1996) also offers a set of basic questions for guiding the process of creating such activity-system maps.

- Is each activity consistent with the overall positioning – the varieties of the products, the needs served, and the type of customers accessed?
- Are there ways to strengthen how activities and groups of activities reinforce one another?
- Could changes in one activity eliminate the need to perform others?

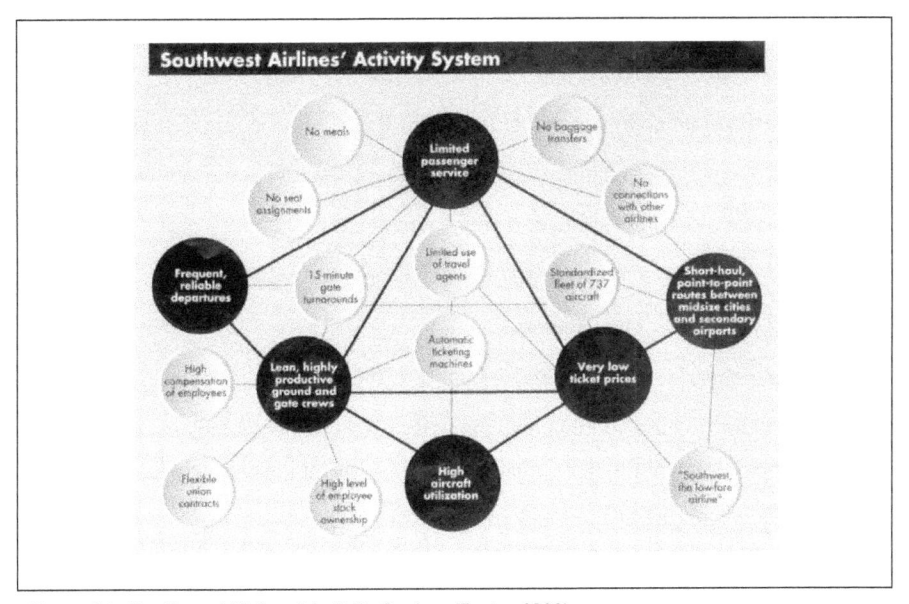

Figure 14 - Southwest Airlines' Activity System (Porter 1996)

Markides (2000) supports Porter's arguments of the existence of synergies in the value chain activities and the interaction of the competencies making the combined whole greater than the separate parts. According to him what makes companies successful are not the individual competencies but the uniqueness of their combination. Furthermore, he offers three principles to follow when putting together the activity system. The individual activities the company chooses to perform must,

(1) Be the ones demanded by the market. The goal is to identify activities that will give a company 'fit' with what the market requires;

(2) Fit together internally; and

(3) Be in balance with one another.

Furthermore, as we shall see in Chapter 3.4 an organizational context and culture has to be created to enable the activity system to stay flexible and responsive to changes in the environment.

The following list summarizes again essential questions when it comes to the redefinition of the business model:

- How do you reach your customers?
- How easy or difficult is it for the customer to find and buy the product?
- How easy is it to do business and interact with your company?
- How aligned are our channels and processes with the needs of the customers?
- How could you achieve a higher degree of interaction with your customers?
- What would be more fun for you and your customers?
- How could you improve the customer's total buying cycle experience?
- How could you reach noncustomers?
- How could create new distribution channels and innovative points of presence?
- How transparent is the information you have available to the customers? Do they have access to vital information, which could enhance their experience?
- Is your price affordable by the mass of buyers?
- How creatively do you work with suppliers, partners, alliances? How could you work with them in such a way that it creates a competitive advantage? Are they an integrated part of your business model?
- How well do your activities fit internally and externally?

- How well do the activities reinforce each other?
- Could you redesign core processes differently to improve efficiency and effectiveness?
- What is the most expensive part of your existing business? How could decrease this cost?
- How can you either perform additional or eliminate unnecessary steps in the value chain?
- Could you eliminate certain steps in your value chain altogether? Or maybe outsource them? Could you outsource them to your customers? (Think IKEA)
- What is the best organizational structure for implementing this strategy?

Table 7 illustrates the tensions of redefining the business model.

conventional customer interface	⇔	(co-creating) experiences easy to do business with
conventional pricing (either to cover cost or benchmarked against competitors)	⇔	strategic pricing of the masses (benchmarked against substitutes and alternative industries)
cost-plus thinking	⇔	price-minus thinking target costs
integrate activities	⇔	network (with customers, suppliers, partners, alliances)
low fit of activities (internally and externally)	⇔	high fit of activities (internally and externally)

Table 7 - Redefining the Business Model

Content dimensions of strategic innovation

Although the content of strategic innovation has been illustrated in a logical sequence, and business, customer, product and business model, respectively technology issues have been discussed separately, it should be clear that all these dimensions are closely related to each other and highly interdependent. Changes in one dimension are likely to entail changes in the other dimensions as well.

We have also seen that certain issues, like the question of assets and capabilities, can have an influence on the business definition, the customer chosen, the product, and the business model and therefore cannot be considered in a vacuum. As pointed out earlier Davenport, Leibold et al (2006) criticize the assumption of linearity of strategic management, arguing that in practice the process and issues are rather diffuse, on-going and intertwining. Thus, when it comes to strategic innovation, such interdependence should be welcomed. Even though it may be unsatisfying and one might feel uncomfortable, it is the nature of real life in general and strategic management in particular. The challenge is to build organizations being capable of handling this ambiguity.

It seems nevertheless imperative to mention that strategic innovation can happen while looking at the business from any angle. Historically in the 1980s, companies were told to start thinking about strategy by looking at the industry and the market (Porter's five forces). In the early 1990s, the resourced-based view of the firm became popular and companies were told to start by looking at what they do best and which core competencies they possess. In the late 1990s, it became popular to understand customer needs and finding ways for creating superior value for customers. Markides points out that all of these approaches are valid and useful ways of developing strategy, because "...creative ideas emerge when we force our mind to start its thinking at different starting points" (Mang 2000). Maybe one has a good idea for a new customer to target through a traditional channel or with the conventional product. Maybe the company has developed a great new product and now needs to think about whom to sell it to. The essence is to approach the issues involved and start the thinking process from different angles and use as many points of views as possible, bearing in mind that it is crucial to challenge the conventional answers and mental models of the industry, the company, managers, and people in the organization.

The content dimensions presented here are meant to offer a framework for thinking thru the issues involved and should spark the thinking process, as well as help to reveal the current industry assumptions and established logic. Your industry is completely local; what would happen if you tried to go global? Does the industry focus on highly functional products; what if you would appeal to consumers' emotions? Competitors keep on adding functionality; what if you started to question the race for the next level and asked the customer what she really needs? Bear in mind that there is no right or wrong answer, but it is always good to start by questioning the current ones. The sources of strategic innovation can be either a new business definition, a new who, a new what, a new how or a combination of all four.

To close this chapter the content dimensions of strategic innovation from the previous chapters are summarized (Table 8) and a tool for assessing strategic innovation is educed.

	Dimension	Benchmark questions
What is your business?	Industry assumptions	What are the main assumptions in your industry? Are they still valid? How can you challenge these?
	Assets and capabilities	Do you let yourself be constrained by the existing assets? How could you creatively leverage existing assets? Or do you need to question existing assets completely and start anew?
Who is your customer?	Customers	Do you focus on existing customers only or do you also target noncustomers?
	Profitability	Do you focus on the most profitable customers, or do you also consider less profitable ones?
	Satisfaction	Do you target the most satisfied customers or the less satisfied?
	Buyers	Does your offering target a single buyer or the chain of buyers?
	Segmentation: differences vs commonalities	How do you segment markets: by differences or by commonalities?
	Segmentation: attributes vs circumstances	Do you segment by consumer or product attributes or by circumstances?
What products and services do you offer?	Product	Do you focus on a single product or a total solution? Is it only a product or an experience?
	Appeal	Do you use a functional or rather emotional appeal?
	Product vs Function	Do you focus on the product or the job-to-be-done?
	Features	Do you keep on improving and adding features or do you selectively raise, reduce, create, and eliminate?
How are you doing this?	Customer interface including distribution channels	Do you rely on conventional channels? Do you offer (co-creation) experiences to customers? Is every step of the buying cycle addressed by the channels? How easy is it to do business with your company?
	Revenue streams and price	Do you benchmark your prices against competition or alternative industries? Is your price affordable to the masses? Do you think cost-plus? Do you have innovative revenue streams?
	Cost	Does your cost structure enable a strategic price targeted at the masses?
	Activity system fit including the network	How well do the activities you carry out balance and reinforce each other? How well do you use the connection to suppliers, partners and alliances?

Table 8 - The Content Dimensions of Strategic Innovation

Mapping strategic innovation

To illustrate the content dimensions in practice, and be able to assess and compare the level of strategic innovation and thereby the differentiation of companies I have developed the "Strategic Innovation Profile", mapping the questions elaborated at the end of each part and from Table 8 above.

The suggestion is to ask the questions mentioned and rate the answers for the companies being compared.

Although the rating is only of a qualitative nature, the outer positions on a scale from one to five are explained below. In general conventional logic, and me too imitation always scores one, while radically different approaches and the complete departure from industry standards scores five.

Additional inspiration for assessing the level in a particular dimension could look like follows:

1 = conventional me too

2 = imitative innovation

3 = slightly innovative; some new ideas; not too risky

4 = innovative; risky new ideas

5 = radically different

As the industry assumptions are further defined by the "who – what – how" dimensions, only these and the assets are used in the profile (Table 9). The issue of integration and outsourcing has been added to the activity system, because even if activities are carried out by suppliers or partners, it is still vital they fit into the activity system as a whole.

	Dimension	Scale	
		1 ⟵⟶ 5	
	approach	*traditional*	*innovative*
Who	Assets	existing assets	new assets
	Customers	existing customers	3rd tier noncustomers
	Profitability	most profitable	least profitable
	Satisfaction	most satisfied	least satisfied
	Segmentation	differences	commonalities
	Buyer	single buyer	chain of buyers
	Attributes vs Circumstances	attributes	circumstances
What	Total Solution	single product	total solution; experiences
	Appeal	according to industry (either functional or emotional)	against conventional logic
	Product vs Function	product	function
	Features	improve and raise	selectively raise, reduce, create, and eliminate
How	Customer interface	conventional logic	experiences; every element of buying cycle addressed
	Revenue streams and pricing	conventional logic	new streams strategic pricing
	Cost	not aligned with strategic price of the masses	aligned with strategic price of the masses
	Activity system	low fit, me too logic	high fit, creative rearrangement of activities

Table 9 - The Scale of the Strategic Innovation Profile

A resulting Strategic Innovation Profile could look like Figure 15 below.

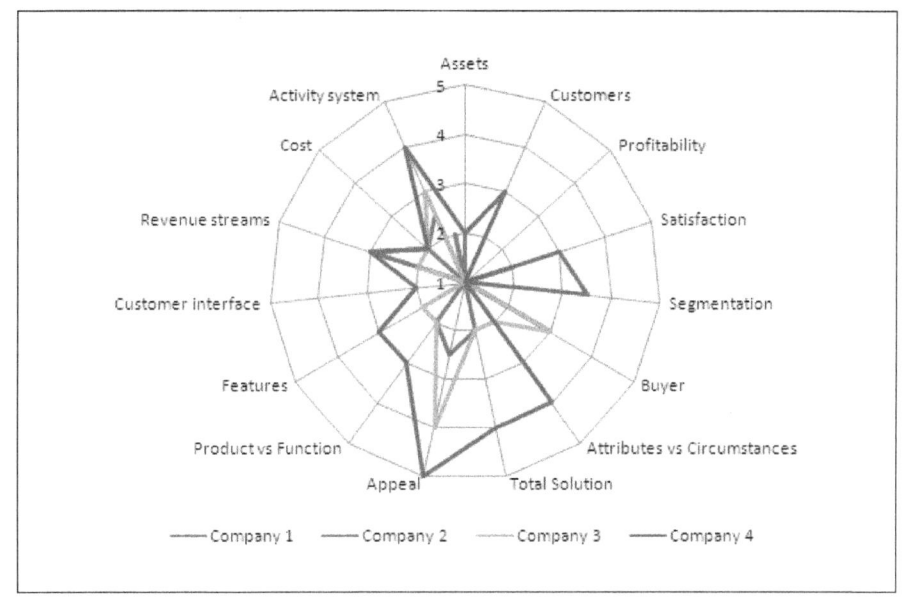

Figure 15 - The Strategic Innovation Profile[5]

The strategic innovation profile can be expanded by incorporating other dimensions considered being important in the particular case. The key is to define what conventional logic within the company or the industry is, and what would be regarded as a departure from that logic and thus an innovation.

In the example above we can clearly see that the players in the industry focus on the most profitable customers, rather on the product than on the function fulfilled, use existing assets and leverage these, while using conventional customer interfaces and distribution channels.

When done by different people in house the profile can also reveal the different mental models and help to create a shared picture of the current situation.

Mapping the strategic profile of an industry or key rivals not only visualizes how innovative the industry or a company's strategy is, but can also help identifying areas for innovation.

---

[5] The development of this profile was inspired by Sawhney's (Sawhney, Wolcott et al. 2006) „innovation radar".

In the example above further potential for differentiation might lie in the profitability, assets, customer interface and cost dimensions, where companies from the example hit the same score.

The next chapter will deal with the process of strategic innovation, namely with how to develop innovative ideas in the potential content dimensions identified.

5. The Process of Strategic Innovation

"Strategic thinking is in its very essence questioning, challenging, unconventional, and innovative."

(Bod De Wit and Ron Meyer)

Christensen and Raynor (2003) point out that most "managers are anxious that their strategy be the right one" (Christensen and Raynor 2003), and meanwhile forget to ask about, what they consider a far more important question, the process of strategy formulation. They believe this to be the reason many businesses end up with flawed strategies.

According to De Wit and Meyer (2004) the strategy process can be dissected into three partially overlapping issues:

(1) **Strategic thinking** focusing on the *strategist* and the question how managers should organize their thinking to achieve a successful strategic reasoning process.

(2) **Strategy formation** focusing on the *strategy* and the question how managers should organize the strategizing activities to achieve a successful strategy formation process.

(3) **Strategic change** focusing on the *organization* and the question of how change should be organized to achieve a successful strategic renewal process.

When it comes to strategic thinking the fundamental question is how managers "…can escape getting stuck with an outdated cognitive map. How can they avoid the danger of building up a flawed picture of their industry, their markets, and themselves? As strategists must be acutely aware of unfolding opportunities and threats in the environment, and the evolving strengths and weaknesses of the organization, they must be able to constantly re-evaluate their views. On the one hand, this requires rigorous logical thinking. On the other hand, strategists must have the ability to engage in creative thinking." (De Wit and Meyer 2004)

As we have seen above it is not only the managers' mental models that need to be challenged, but those of the entire organization as such.

Regarding strategy formation, two main schools of thought can be identified: those seeing strategy as a planned and intended course of action and those believing strategy being a realized course of action. Whereas the first school is forward looking the second is retrospective.

Mintzberg (1987; 1994) has observed that strategy is both: it is intended and deliberate, while it is also emergent, all of these elements finally defining the realized strategy (Figure 16).

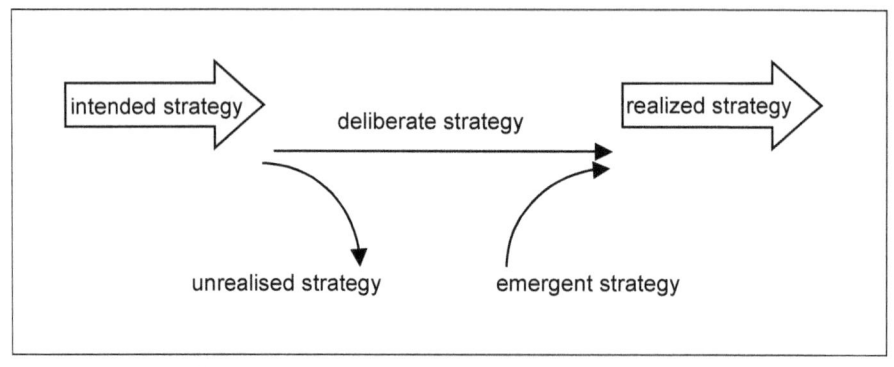

Figure 16 - Types of Strategies (Mintzberg and Waters 1985)

On the subject of strategic change, again two opposite views can be observed: change being either revolutionary (disruptive, radical) or evolutionary (gradual, incremental). According to De Wit and Meyer (2004) it is widely accepted among researchers that companies need to balance both, however most authors seeing the balance between revolutionary strategic change and evolutionary operational change.

Chakravarthy and White (2002) have criticized that strategy process research has currently too many limitations and is, basically, too narrow. They put forward a more holistic approach linking the strategy process to desired outcomes, putting it into the business and organizational context, while taking into consideration the company's present performance and its ability to learn over time.

Being aware of these limitations, the current chapter will focus on the particular formation process of innovative strategies, the outcomes of which have been identified above as new business models, new markets and value improvements.

The underlining assumption being that the current business and organization is determined largely by the management's cognitive maps and the organization's mental models, the process should enable to challenge these. As we shall see learning thru experimentation will play an important role in the process. The current performance of the organization will not be taken into consideration. Furthermore, as a detailed description would go beyond the scope of this study, I will focus on providing an overview of the process on a high level and outline the key success factors of each step.

As we have seen while defining strategy and strategic management in general, an important element is choice. In order to be able to make choices options are needed.

Thus, the first step is to generate a maximum of options, from which the company can choose. According to Markides, "this is exactly where innovation in strategy comes into play. The more creative a firm can be at this "idea-generation" stage, the higher the probability that it will end up with an innovative strategy – one that breaks the rules of the game" (Markides 1999), a belief shared by Hamel (1998; 1998). After the options have been generated, ideas need to be evaluated and chosen from. Finally the chosen strategy needs to be implemented (Markides 1999; Markides 2000).

Hamel (1998) also proposes a similar three step process, consisting of (1) discovery, (2) synthesis, and (3) experimentation, for developing strategy.

Hansen and Birkinshaw (2007) have developed what they call the innovation value chain; a end-to-end process consisting of the three steps (1) idea generating, (2) conversion, and (3) diffusion.

Levitt (2002) argues that there is a difference between creativity and innovation. While to him it seems easy to be creative and generate many ideas, being innovative and implementing these ideas with businesslike follow-through is more difficult.

Leonard and Straus (1997), as well as Bragg and Bragg (2005) call the discovery phase divergent, and the synthesis phase the convergent phase. First companies need to have divergent discussions to generate alternatives, followed by a convergent discussion to select an option and plan its implementation.

Kim and Mauborgne (2002; 2005) suggest instead of preparing dense documents filled with numbers, as it is the case with traditional strategic planning, to build the process around a picture to visualize the result and enhance the discussion. They also suggest starting the strategizing process by visualizing the current strategy first.

Christensen (1997) also advocates to start strategy making by identifying and visually mapping the driving forces in the competitive environment.

Thus, following the ideas of these authors, I propose the following process steps for strategic innovation:

(1) Visualizing and describing the current strategy

(2) Generating new ideas

(3) Evaluating and testing these new ideas

(4) Choosing and implementing the new strategy.

Furthermore, considering the argument that creativity is not innovation, and that divergent and convergent discussions are need, each focusing on very specific objectives, it is suggested to split the four steps and associated activities into two phases:

(1) An exploration phase, focusing on broadening the option space, and consisting of the steps (1) visualization and (2) generation;

(2) An execution phase, focusing on narrowing the option space, consisting of the steps (3) assessment and (4) implementation.

The process suggested here can be applied on both, the strategic thinking and the strategy formation level as defined by De Wit and Meyer (2004) and described beforehand.

The four steps will be discussed in more detail in the remaining parts of this chapter, which will close with a summarizing graphic illustration of the process and associated steps.

Visualizing and describing the current strategy

The goal of this first step is to identify the existing mental models, of both the people involved in the strategy formulation process, at this first step primarily top management, and the company. Senge (1996) argues that learning can only take place, once we are aware of our mental models and are able to express and discuss them, which is only possible if participants have a common picture. Furthermore, this step also helps identifying industry assumptions, the established base of competition, and opportunities for strategic innovation.

Kim and Mauborgne (2002; 2005) call this first step "visual awakening" and suggest it serves three main objectives:

(1) It enables to resolve differences of opinion about the current stage of play;

(2) It serves as a wake-up call, illustrating the need for change, making a stronger case than any argument based on numbers and words could do;

(3) It facilitates a common understanding of the company's current strategy, position and what top management considers being competitive factors.

Whereas drawing the strategy canvas as proposed by Kim and Mauborgne will help identifying the main competitive elements concerning the offering, drawing the strategic innovation profile developed above will illustrate a more holistic picture of the content dimensions to consider.

Thus, the suggestion to start with developing the strategic innovation profile, followed by a deep dive into the current offerings with the aid of the strategy canvas. The picture can be further completed by outlining all business activities on an activities system map as described by Porter and testing them in regard to their fit.

Visualizing and describing the current strategy using the new, and unfamiliar instruments, will make people in the organization acquainted to them and create a common understanding of the new instruments, the content dimensions involved, and the company's strategy and thus build a common language for discussing strategy, an element Mankins and Steele (2005) consider being among the most important success factors of strategic management. The visual representation of the current state furthermore helps to debate assumptions, instead of forecasts as is usually the case during traditional strategic planning sessions and thus "...frees management from the tyranny of numbers" (Christensen 1997).

Although most authors on strategic innovation dismiss the conventional analytical first step of industry or SWOT analysis when it comes to strategizing for reasons outlined before, traditional tools, being aware of their limitations, could be used to generate further insight into what factors influence competition or how customers perceive the different offerings, and which criteria they rely on to make the buying decision for example.

Depending on the number of people involved in this first step, individual managers can be asked to draw their version of the two graphics, or they could be split into different teams during a workshop for example. As outlined earlier, the content dimensions are particular useful on the business unit level, thus different graphics could be developed by different teams for various units, or various regions.

Results should then be compared to illustrate differences in prevailing mental models. This knowledge could be further enhanced by asking customers, suppliers, industry experts, and maybe even competitors, what they consider being industry norms, key factors of competition and how they would rank each player's level.

Having outlined these maps of the conventional, established thinking one can start questioning and challenging the answers given, following the next process steps outlined below.

Generating ideas

"Imagination is more important than knowledge."

(Albert Einstein)

The goal of the second step is to generate as many new and creative options as possible. According to Sutton, "to find a few ideas that work, you need to try a lot that don't" (LaBarre 2002). The question arising is how this can be enabled.

The literature on idea generation and creativity is vast, ranging from the traditional approaches of brainstorming, or creative and lateral thinking as outlined for example by de Bono (1996), to more innovative ways, such as toolkits for user innovation described above or techniques like TRIZ, a systematic process for product innovation.

Although managers and those in charge of strategy development or facilitating such processes are encouraged to familiarize themselves with these techniques, a complete presentation would clearly go beyond the scope of this study. Table 10 on the next page gives an overview of common idea generation techniques.

Nevertheless some elements that are considered being especially useful to the crafting of innovative strategies will be discussed with a focus on idea generation in the context of business and strategic innovation in particular and considering primarily authors writing on strategic innovation or business creativity.

Technique	Examples
Checklists	• Davis • Osborne • SCAMPER • Big four • Customer journey
Upside-down thinking	• Rule reversal • Assumption reversal
Analogical thinking	• Bionics • Underlying principles • Business processes • Sub-systems & components
Free association	• Brainstorming • Mind-Mapping
Combinations	• Morphological analysis • Force-fitting
Stimulus material	• Words • Pictures • Objects

Table 10 - Idea Generation Techniques (adapted from Bragg and Bragg 2005)

Ideas for strategic innovation can come from a variety of external and internal sources.

Linder, Davenport et al. (2003) list for example the following five external innovation sourcing channels:

- Buying innovation on the market through sponsored research, innovation for hire, strategic procurement;
- Investing in innovators through venture capital, or equity partnerships;
- Co sourcing with competitors within or across innovation sectors, or through joint-ventures;
- Sourcing from communities of sophisticated users (open source for example);
- Resourcing on-demand talent and innovative new tools.

According to Nambisan and Sawhney (2007) external sources can range from buying raw ideas, to market ready ideas and market ready products. Whereas raw ideas are regarded as being cheaper, speed is also low, while risk is high. On the other hand the risk when buying market ready products is very low, whereas speed, but also cost are high. They also suggest that outside sourcing is most useful when the internal innovation portfolio is weak.

Wolpert (2002) advocates companies should make innovation a natural element of commerce and exchange innovations through independent intermediaries. Ideas could thus be bought on an open market.

Kao (1996) adds that outsiders can also be hired on a just-in-time basis to increase the variety.

Hansen and Birkinshaw (2007) argue that cross-unit collaboration is very often overlooked as a source for generating ideas. They distinguish between (1) in-house idea generation, i.e. inside functional groups or business units, (2) cross-unit collaboration, i.e. combining insights and knowledge from different parts of the same company, and (3) outside sources, namely outside the company, but also outside the industry.

As we have seen while discussing the content dimensions of strategic innovation other outside channels can include competitors, other industries, other countries etc.

Traditional strategic planning workshops are an example of a typical internal source for generating ideas.

Although, as "...innovation takes place when different ideas, perceptions and ways of processing and judging information collide, [which], in turn, often requires collaboration among various players who see the world in inherently different ways" (Leonard and Straus 1997), traditional planning workshops featuring only top management might have their limitations in challenging established assumptions.

In order to achieve the necessary variety, the first step is to ask a large number of people throughout the organization to contribute to the process. Ideally everybody should be involved, as the discovery phase has to be carried out all the way through the organization as a whole (Hamel 1998).

A broad involvement of the entire company, also results in what Kim and Mauborgne (2005) call "a fair process", making the emotional buy-in, commitment and thereby the implementation of the resulting strategy easier. Tushman and O'Reilly (1997) agree that motivation and commitment are important, and can be established only if people believe their efforts contribute to some higher good and make a difference.

According to Tushman and O'Reilly (1997) commitment can be created through a participative process with the three characteristics (1) choice, (2) visibility of activities and collaboration, and (3) irrevocability of decisions, each of them making decisions more binding.

Such an involvement of the entire company could be achieved by using a typical suggestion box, message boards on the intranet, establishing virtual communities, or markets for ideas, providing the best ones with venture capital (Yates and Skarzynski 1999; Hamel and Välikangas 2003), or real time strategic change and open space conferences.

However, not only do companies need a large number of committed people; they also need to make sure that the people as such represent a multitude of viewpoints and approaches.

Many authors on business creativity and strategic innovation explicitly state the need for a large variety in people, bringing in new and unconventional voices (1996; Kao 1996; Leonard and Straus 1997; Hamel 1998; Beinhocker 1999; Eisenhardt 1999; Kim and Mauborgne 1999; Markides 1999; Markides 1999; Yates and Skarzynski 1999; Markides 2000; Abraham and Knight 2001; Sutton 2001), young people, as well as people from the organization's geographic periphery, the argument being, the further away one is from headquarters, the less resource one has, and thus is forced to be more creative (Hamel 1996; Hamel 1998).

Tushman (1997) explicitly states the importance of keeping the senior executive team relatively young and diverse. He furthermore states the time an executive team is in place having an impact on the performance of the company. Very young teams do not do well, just as performance declines when teams become older. Teams seem to peak at an average age of 3.5 years.

A diversity of experience, age, sex, race, national origin, and so forth is considered being crucial (Beinhocker 1999).

According to Pearson (2002) most successful innovations require the following key participants:

- A champion who believes that the new idea is really critical and who will keep pushing ahead, no matter what the roadblocks;
- A sponsor who is high up enough in the organization to marshal its resources, people, money, and time;
- A mix of bright, creative minds to get ideas;
- Experienced operators to keep things practical.

Ziegler (2002) argues that there is no single job description for innovators. Moreover, being an innovator does not mean behaving in just one way. There are different aspects to innovation, and people in an organization can all be innovators by playing different roles. He suggests the following ones:

- "The Dreamer. This is the person with the faraway look in her eyes; sometimes it appears that she isn't thinking at all. What she's actually doing, however, is gazing into the future, connecting a lot of disparate things and asking, "What if . . . ?"
- The Spark Plug. He's the guy with more energy than he knows what to do with, the idea guy, making new connections in the here and now: "Look, here's how this could be done better, faster, easier."
- The Planner. The Spark Plug isn't of much use without the Planner. This is the receptive listener, the "fertile soil" on which the seed of an idea falls. She knows how to link ideas and resources ("You should go talk to . . . "). She thinks about a business case; she knows where to find the money and people to make it all happen.
- The Implementer. Here is your classic sponsor or champion. He takes the plans and makes it happen: builds the house, digs the canal, sells the products and services. He manages a project, measures progress and ensures that the benefits are realized.

The point of thinking about these roles is not to get carried away with only the Spark Plugs or the Dreamers, the Planners or the Implementers. Each role is vital. A company made up of only idea people can never be anything more than potentially innovative." (Ziegler 2002)

When it comes to variety in people, Kelley (2005) probably offers the most complete categorization describing ten possible roles of innovation team members. He points out that not all ten are required on every team and that people can occupy multiple roles, but the variety will expand the overall potential and broaden the horizon.

As we can see, many of the suggestions on where to look for new answers to the content questions identified beforehand are covered by Kelley's personas (Table 11).

Personas	Role	Description
The **Learning** Personas Constantly gather information from new sources, keep the team from becoming too internally focused, question their own worldview.	Anthropologist	Brings new learning and insights by observing human behavior and developing a deep understanding of how people interact physically and emotionally with products, services, and spaces.
	Experimenter	Prototypes new ideas continuously, learning by a process of enlightened trial and error.
	Cross-Pollinator	Explores other industries and cultures, then translates those findings and revelations to fit the unique needs of the company.
The **Organizing** Personas Savvy about the counterintuitive process of how organizations move ideas forward.	Hurdler	Knows the path to innovations is strewn with obstacles and develops a knack for overcoming those roadblocks.
	Collaborator	Helps bring eclectic groups together, and often leads the middle of the pack to create new combinations and multidisciplinary solutions.
	Director	Gathers a talented cast and crew, helps to spark their creative talents.
The **Building** Personas Apply insights from the learning roles and channel the empowerment from the organizing personas to make innovation happen.	Experience Architect	Designs compelling experiences to connect at a deeper level with customers' latent or expressed needs.
	Set Designer	Creates a stage on which innovation team members can do their best work, transforming physical environments into powerful tools to influence behavior and attitude.
	Caregiver	Builds on the metaphor of a health care professional to deliver customer care in a manner that goes beyond mere service.
	Storyteller	Builds both internal morale and external awareness through compelling narratives that communicate a fundamental human value or reinforce a specific cultural trait.

Table 11 - The Ten Faces of Innovation (following Kelley 2005)

In order to make innovation an ongoing process such a variety of voices needs to be available internally (Markides 1999; Markides 2000). This can be achieved by hiring, working with and promoting people, who "make oneself uncomfortable" (Leonard and Straus 1997; Sutton 2001).

Sutton (2001) suggests to hire slow learners, who do not adapt too fast to the "way things are done around here", newcomers who do not know how things are supposed to be, people with high self-esteem, who can act and think independently, misfits and mavericks, who do not care about how to act. He also suggests, as creativity is a function of the quantity of work produced, to reward success and failure, while punishing inaction.

Govindarajan and Trimble (2006) argue that it is crucial to hire outsiders to manage new ventures, as they are not biased by the mental models of the current business.

Levitt (2002) suggests to have a special group, whose function is to receive ideas, work them out and follow them through in the necessary manner. In the case of strategy, the office of strategic management or a head of strategic innovation and her team could carry out this task.

To win the most promising and interested talents for such teams and for new projects, internal markets for talents could be established (Hamel and Välikangas 2003; Bryan and Joyce 2005) or professionals could be asked to sign up for a particular project or for working with a particular team or manager (Kelley 2001).

Markides (2000) and Hamel (1998) point out that while generating ideas is the responsibility of the entire company, choosing which ideas to pursue, the synthesis and evaluation of the ideas, has to be done by top management bearing the overall responsibility.

In order to choose, ideas need to be evaluated.

Evaluating ideas

"On s'engage et puis on voit."

(Napoléon Bonaparte)

Common brainstorming knowledge recommends the evaluation of ideas being separated from the generation stage. This seems also important in the context of strategic innovation. If ideas are evaluated while being developed, they are likely to be dismissed as being impossible, not realistic, etc. Thus, to avoid this early criticism, it is suggested to separate the two steps.

For an initial evaluation of the ideas generated, the tools elaborated above, namely the strategy canvas, the strategic innovation profile and the according questions, can be used. Drawing these two graphics will show whether the ideas are truly unconventional and bear the potential for strategic innovation. Furthermore, it is expected that management will know which ideas constitute a departure from conventional logic.

After such an initial assessment, management must decide which ideas to pursue and test further to gain new insights and see what works and what does not and whether the new strategy is adopted by the market or not. The aim is to screen, provide initial funding, and come from the raw idea to first results (Hansen and Birkinshaw 2007).

In regard to decision making, Mintzberg and Westley (2001) have identified the three decision-making approaches (1) "thinking first", (2) "seeing first", and (3) "doing first". Whereas "thinking first" is most appropriate in a structured context, where reliable data is available and the issue is clear, "seeing first" has to be applied when many elements have to be combined into creative solutions. Finally "doing first" is most suitable in novel and confusing situations, where complicated specifications would get in the way and a few simple relationship rules can help people move forward.

As the resulting outcomes of strategic innovation are supposed to be completely new and a departure from the conventional logic and way of doing business, no data is likely to exist. The strategy and its outcomes are highly uncertain, therefore, no amount of prior analysis can resolve these unknowns, only experimentation and learning can (Govindarajan and Trimble 2004). While "doing" these strategic experiments, management will "see" what works in the market place and has the potential for success and what does not.

Handy (1980) agrees by saying that normal planning procedures do not apply when so many parameters are unknown. "One can only proceed by trial and error, by controlled experiment, by hedging one's bets, by fanning the sparks of success, and by quickly abandoning the ashes of failure." (Handy 1980)

Markides (2000) and Webber (2000) add experimenting with different ideas being more productive and outperforming the conduction of extensive analysis and discussion. Markides (2000) also argues that the development of superior strategy is part planning and part trial and error.

Furthermore organizations learn by trying new things and by engaging in these experiments (Huy and Mintzberg 2003).

The idea of strategic experimentation is supported by many authors, arguing that experimentation, trial and error, or prototyping a new product, service or strategy is the only possibility to really see whether it has the potential for success and is being accepted by the market or not (Hamel 1996; Lynn, Morone et al. 1996; Markides 1997; Hamel 1998; Markides 1999; Markides 1999; Pascale 1999; Kawasaki 2000; Koch 2000; Liedtka 2000;

Markides 2000; Webber 2000; Kelley 2001; Loewe, Williamson et al. 2001; Beinhocker and Kaplan 2002; Christensen and Raynor 2003; Huy and Mintzberg 2003; Peters 2003; Godin 2004; Govindarajan and Trimble 2004; Hamel and Getz 2004; Leonard and Swap 2004; Govindarajan and Trimble 2005).

Whereas Markides (1997; 2000) suggests to experiment in a limited way or area, defined by top management, Hamel and Välikangas (2003), Pearson (2002), as well as Huy and Mintzberg (2003) suggest companies should engage in a multitude of small experiments involving low risk. Pearson (2002) argues that this multitude encourages more risk taking since people do not expect every experiment to succeed. It contains costs since tests and trials do not get expand until they show real promise and it improves the odds of success because "you're betting on a portfolio, not on one or two big, long-odds projects" (Pearson 2002). Beinhocker (1999) supports the argument that, because of the future being uncertain, it is important to have more strategic experiments going on in parallel.

Beinhocker (1999; 1999) even suggests that strategy be a portfolio of diverse strategic experiments. Companies should cultivate and manage a population of strategies that evolve over time. He furthermore agrees with Pearson that parallelism in experiments has several benefits:

- "Innovation and progress require experiments, yet experiments are risky; parallelism in experiments increases the odds that one or more will work out.
- What is fit today may not be fit tomorrow; having a population of strategies allows some diversity, which increases the odds of survival when the environment changes.
- Parallelism breeds boldness; having multiple experiments allows you to take a few risks without 'betting the farm'." (Beinhocker 1999)

Beinhocker (1999) also puts forward the idea of categorizing the portfolio of experiments along the three dimensions time (payoffs in the near, medium, or long term), risk (low, medium, or high), and aim (expanding or defending a current business, building a new one that has already been identified, or laying the foundations for potential new businesses). Such a categorization could be used to assess the innovation pipeline of the company. A balanced mix of experiments in each area should be aspired.

In order to enable real learning from these strategic experiments, they should be designed to test very specific hypotheses about where future opportunities may be found (Beinhocker and Kaplan 2002).

Govindarajan and Trimble (2004) support this argument by stating that learning can only happen if the people involved share a common story about how the experiment is expected to work, which requires to focus on the assumptions underlying expected outcomes and predictions, instead of focusing on the predictions themselves and to communicate in detail the theory used to generate the predictions. In addition, they suggest focusing on a small number of unknowns, e.g. most critical market, technology, cost unknown, instead of focusing on too many details with a business plan for example.

Christensen and Raynor (2003), as well as McGrath and MacMillan (1995) point out that the assumptions about outcomes are often biased by the way things worked in the past. In order to keep track of the underlying assumptions a checklist covering the content dimensions of strategic innovation could be put together. The discussion can then revolve around these assumptions instead of the financial outcomes, as everybody knows they must look good anyhow (McGrath and MacMillan 1995; Christensen and Raynor 2003).

For strategic experiments to be valuable and enable true learning and new insights, some key success factors have to be observed.

Thomke (2001) defines experimentation as the systematic testing of ideas, and puts forward, what he calls "the essentials of enlightened experimentation":

- Organize for rapid experimentation (small development groups, perform in parallel);
- Fail early and often, but avoid mistakes. Embrace failures that occur early in the development process and advance knowledge significantly. Do not forget the basics for experimentation: Well-designed tests have clear objectives (what do you anticipate learning?) and hypotheses (what do you expect to happen?);
- Anticipate and exploit early information (identify problems upstream, where they are easier and cheaper to solve);
- Combine new and traditional technologies.

Govindarajan and Trimble (2005) argue that strategic innovation proceeds with strategic experiments, having the following ten characteristics:

- "They require departure from the corporation's proven business definition as well as its assumptions about what makes a business successful (i.e., they require forgetting).
- They leverage some of the existing assets and capabilities of the corporation (i.e., they require borrowing – they are not simply financial investments in startups).
- They are not simply product-line extensions, geographic expansions, or technological improvements that enhance proven businesses.
- They target emerging and poorly defined industries created by non-linear shifts in the industry environment.
- They are launched before any competitor has proved itself, and when there is no clear formula for making a profit.
- They have very high potential for revenue growth (for example, 10x over 3-5 years).
- They require development of at least some new knowledge and capabilities.
- They are led by general managers who face multiple dimensions of uncertainty across multiple functions. Potential customers are often mere possibilities. Value propositions are often just guesses, because customers themselves have yet to figure out exactly what they want. The value chain and underlying technologies for delivering the new products or services are often unproven.
- They are expected to remain unprofitable for several quarters or more. They are too expensive to repeat.
- It can remain difficult to know whether the experiment is succeeding or failing for several quarters. Feedback is delayed and ambiguous." (Govindarajan and Trimble 2005)

These characteristics can also be used to evaluate the ideas in the first place to make a decision which ones to pursue.

To ensure learning happens it is necessary to review the predictions and outcomes of the strategic experiments on a monthly basis, or even more often if necessary, instead of the traditional yearly strategic planning session (Govindarajan and Trimble 2004).

Drawing on the above said, the following graphic (Figure 17) proposes a structured approach to evaluating strategic ideas.

The Process of Strategic Innovation

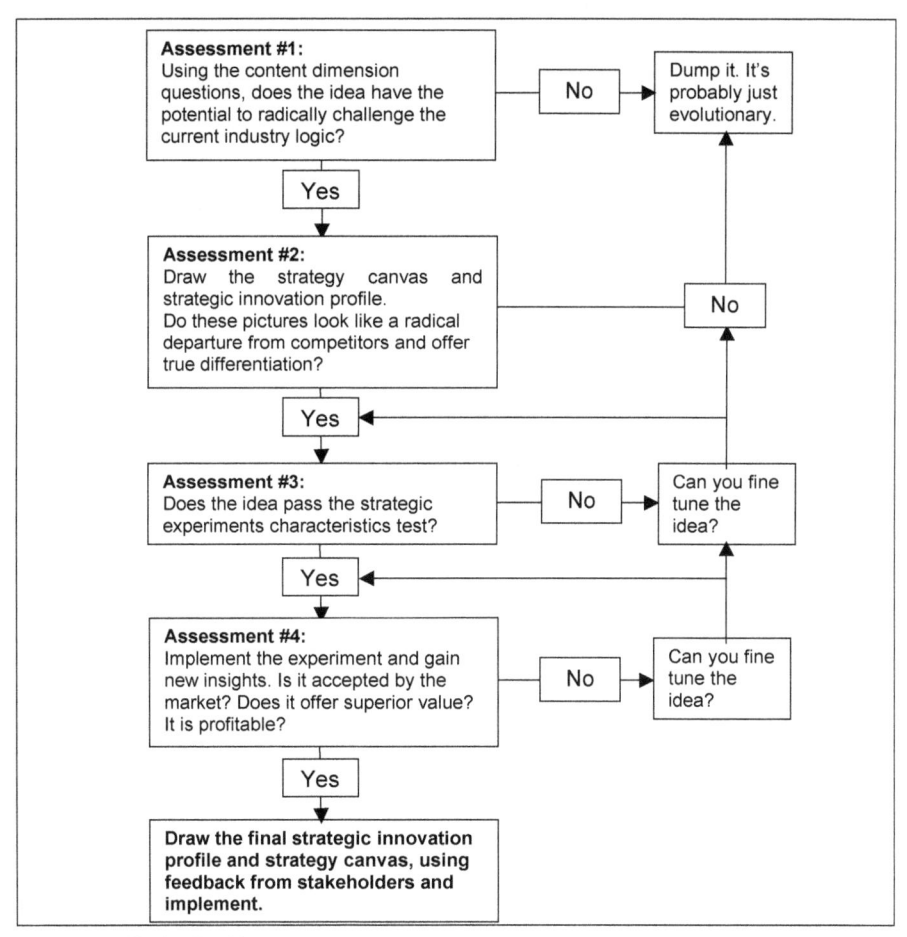

```
┌─────────────────────────────────────┐
│ Assessment #1:                      │
│ Using the content dimension         │──No──▶ Dump it. It's
│ questions, does the idea have the   │        probably just
│ potential to radically challenge the│        evolutionary.
│ current industry logic?             │
└─────────────────────────────────────┘
              │ Yes
              ▼
┌─────────────────────────────────────┐
│ Assessment #2:                      │
│ Draw the strategy canvas and        │
│ strategic innovation profile.       │──No──▶
│ Do these pictures look like a radical│
│ departure from competitors and offer│
│ true differentiation?               │
└─────────────────────────────────────┘
              │ Yes
              ▼
┌─────────────────────────────┐     ┌──────────────┐
│ Assessment #3:              │     │ Can you fine │
│ Does the idea pass the strategic│──No──▶│ tune the   │
│ experiments characteristics test? │     │ idea?        │
└─────────────────────────────┘     └──────────────┘
              │ Yes
              ▼
┌─────────────────────────────┐     ┌──────────────┐
│ Assessment #4:              │     │ Can you fine │
│ Implement the experiment and gain│──No──▶│ tune the   │
│ new insights. Is it accepted by the│     │ idea?        │
│ market? Does it offer superior value?│   └──────────────┘
│ It is profitable?           │
└─────────────────────────────┘
              │ Yes
              ▼
┌─────────────────────────────────────┐
│ Draw the final strategic innovation │
│ profile and strategy canvas, using  │
│ feedback from stakeholders and      │
│ implement.                          │
└─────────────────────────────────────┘
```

Figure 17 - Evaluating Ideas

For a first evaluation the content dimensions' questions can be used. This should give the experienced manager a good overview about whether the idea has the potential to break away from competition and create a new market, new value, or a new business model or not. If the idea does not pass this test, it probably has only evolutionary operational impact.

Next the strategy canvas and strategic innovation profile should be drawn. These will enable a common picture and enhance further discussions. Furthermore they illustrate clearly whether the idea offers the potential for differentiation.

The third step consists of a second round of questions, using the characteristics of strategic experiments. In case a portfolio of strategic experiments is in place, each experiment can be put on a chart using Beinhocker's risk, aim, and time dimensions to see whether the portfolio is balanced. If the majority of experiments scores in the same range as the new one being evaluated, it might be more valuable to consider other alternatives.

The resulting ideas should then be implemented as strategic experiments. These need to be tested on a limited scale. This step entitles allocating the necessary resources, provide funding and a senior manager being in charge of the experiment as we shall see later. The aim of this step is to gain insights and first results, necessary for either pursuing the idea or giving it up.

The final stage involves developing the best future strategy, using feedback from suppliers, customers, competitors' customers, and noncustomers on alternatives (Kim and Mauborgne 2005), before the chosen strategy can be implemented.

Implementing the new strategy

"Men like the opinion to which they have become accustomed from youth; this prevents them from finding the truth, for they cling to the opinion of habit."

(Moses Maimonides)

After the strategic experiments have revealed the ideas to implement, each part not only fits into, but also reinforces the total activity system, and the final strategic innovation profile and strategy canvas have been drawn, the strategy can be executed and implemented into the organization. The goal of this step is to spread the new concept across the organization (Hansen and Birkinshaw 2007). Executing innovative strategies is especially tough because they represent a radical departure from the status quo and the company is likely to face many barriers, hurdles, and blocks.

Whereas the literature on change management (e.g. Kotter 1996) and organizational development offers plenty of advice on how to overcome these barriers, the purpose of this chapter is to create awareness and discuss the most important issues.

The single largest challenge of strategic innovation is to question existing mental models, traditional assumptions, and shifting the company's strategic focus from trying to beat the competition by becoming better, faster, cheaper, to becoming different.

Kim and Mauborgne (2005) have identified four hurdles to execution: cognitive (waking up employees to the need for a change in strategy), limited resources, unmotivated staff, and politics (opposition from powerful interests).

Bragg and Bragg (2005) developed a more extensive list of blocks: human resources, internal and external politics, finances, manufacturing, customers, inability to protect the new idea, competitors, suppliers, regulations, and conventions.

Markides (1998) writes about structural and cultural inertia, internal politics, complacency, fear of destroying existing competencies, fear of cannibalizing existing products, satisfaction with the status quo, and a general lack of incentive to abandon a certain present for an uncertain future as barriers to innovation.

Kotter (1996) identifies complacency being a powerful barrier to change and lists many sources, e.g. the absence of a major and visible crisis, low overall performance standards, organizational structures that focus employees on narrow functional goals, internal measurement systems focusing on the wrong performance measures, a lack of sufficient performance feedback from external sources, a low-confrontation culture, human nature, with its capacity for denial, and too much happy talk from senior management.

As Weick (1996) has demonstrated is it hard for people to "drop their tools" even if they encounter the risk of dying. Weick lists many reasons for this behavior among them that the order might not have been heard, the urgency for the change is not understood, social dynamics, and the fact that people might not know how to forget what they have learned or might not be skilled in the replacement activity.

Govindarajan and Trimble (2005; 2005; 2006) share the argument of forgetting and learning being important for making new ventures successful.

We have already seen above that a fair process, i.e. the involvement of the company as a whole can create employees' buy-in up front (Kim and Mauborgne 2005). Apart from this engagement, Kim and Mauborgne (2005) emphasize the importance of explaining why the final strategic decisions were made and what the expectations in regard to the new goals, new targets, new milestones and responsibilities are.

Kaplan and Norton (1992), Markides (2000), as well as and Kim and Mauborgne (2005) stress the importance of communication in executing strategy and leading change (Kotter 1996). If people have to implement a strategy, they need to know not only what the strategy is, but also how they can contribute to its execution, i.e. they have to be educated and the strategy needs to be explained, not only communicated, accordingly.

The strategic innovation profile, the strategy canvas and a picture of the activity system can be used to communicate the new strategy appropriately. To reinforce the message, before-and-after strategic profiles should be distributed and only projects and steps aiming at closing the gap between the two profiles should be supported (Kim and Mauborgne 2005). Christensen (1997) adds that a specific plan defining how money, manpower and other resources must be allocated to implement the strategy has to be developed.

Markides (1998; 2000) also suggests to create a positive crisis to stimulate the need for change and the abandonment of outdated mental models. Such a positive crisis can be achieved by (1) communicating and explaining what needs to be done, and why, (2) setting new and demanding objectives, which are realistic and achievable, but nevertheless ambitious and stretching, and (3) moving from rational acceptance of the objective to emotional commitment. The argument of creating a sense of urgency by pointing out the need for change, identifying and discussing crises, potential crises, or major opportunities is shared by Hamel and Prahalad (1989), as well as Kotter (1996). Tushman and O'Reilly (1997) suggest emphasizing speed and urgency does promote implementation.

The need for change can also be demonstrated by comparing the current financial health to the strategic health of the corporation (Markides 1998; Markides 2000). Strategic health being an indicator for future financial success, it measures leading indicators such as customer satisfaction, loyalty, market share, employee morale, staff turnover, communication, trends in financial health, innovation and new products in the pipeline, product quality, flexibility, distributor and supplier feedback, quality of the management team, strength of company culture, and so on (Markides 2000).

What makes strategic innovation even harder is the necessity of continuous innovation (e.g. Hamel 1996; Markides 1997; Tushman 1997; Tushman and O'Reilly III 1997; Hamel 1998; Hamel 1998; Markides 1999; Markides 2000; Hamel and Välikangas 2003; Kim and Mauborgne 2005). Implementing an innovative strategy just once, is not enough. Long term success has to do with managing streams of innovation rather than singular innovation events (Tushman 1997) and developing an innovative, successful strategy is a never ending quest (Markides 2000).

While Grant (1991) emphasizes mainly imitation by competitors, Hamel and Välikangas (2003) offer four reasons for the need for constantly innovating on the strategic level: strategies get replicated by competitors; good strategies get supplanted by better ones; they get exhausted as markets become saturated; and strategies get eviscerated by the increasing knowledge and bargaining power of customers.

As we shall see in the next chapter, being innovative on a constant basis requires very specific capabilities that need to be established within the organization.

Considering the above said, the following, resulting process of strategic innovation is proposed (Figure 18).

Visualizing strategy
- strategy canvas
- strategic innovation profile
- describe the strategy
- build a common picture and language
- discuss the strategy
- identify possible areas for innovation

Generating ideas
- generate as many ideas as possible
- using external & internal sources
- involving a variety of people and views

Implementing ideas
- address the barriers
- demonstrate the need for change
- involvement
- communication
- learning and forgetting
- sense of urgency

Evaluating ideas
- using the structured approach
- strategic experimentation

The Process of Strategic Innovation

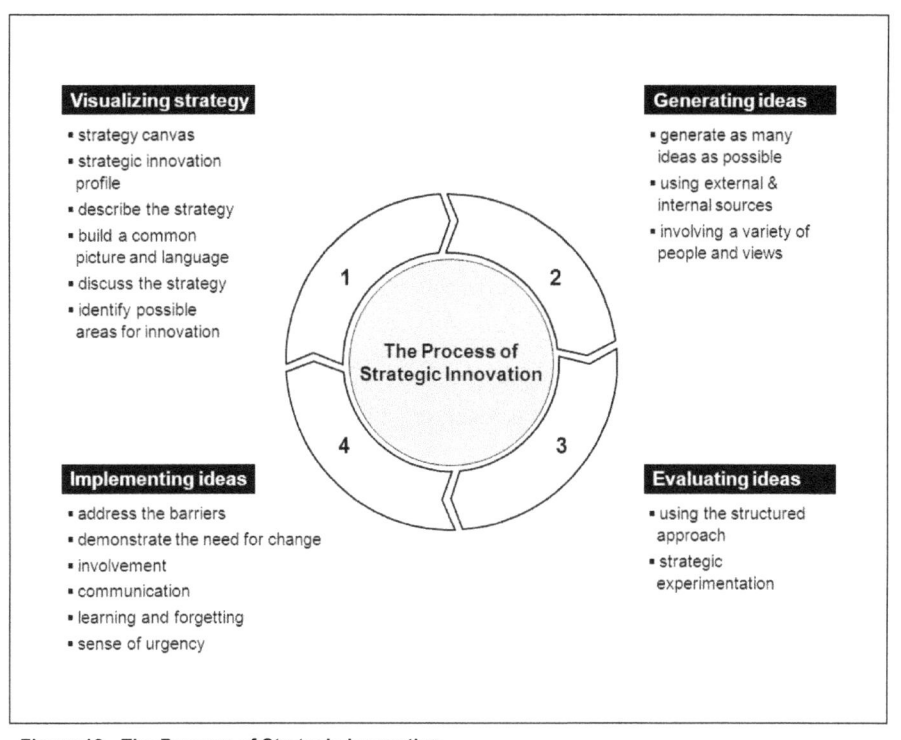

Figure 18 - The Process of Strategic Innovation

Earlier, we have identified two main areas of criticism about the traditional strategic planning processes in companies: (1) strategic planning usually being nothing more than an incremental adaptation of last year's plan, and (2) the planning process being too formal and analytical.

The process developed here is clearly a departure from the incremental approach, as it favors the use of creativity, variety, pictures, and strategic experiments instead of formal planning and budgeting relying on financials only.

Hansen and Birkinshaw (2007) suggest companies should assess which of the steps on the innovation value chain they are best at, the argument being that very often companies think of themselves as being poor innovators, because they think that they do not generate enough creative ideas for example, when in reality they lack the necessary skills for diffusion. The following self-assessment tool (Figure 19) can help to identify the areas in need of improvement.

In order to assess an organization's level of strategic innovativeness the following process questions could be added to the strategic innovation profile.

- Who is in charge of developing new ideas? Only top management or the organization as a whole, i.e. everybody?
- How diverse is the strategic management team and those contributing the ideas? Think of experience, age, sex, race, national origin, Kelley's personas, etc.
- When does strategic planning and assessment take place? Once a year or continuously?
- Do strategic discussions revolve around the financial outcomes and the business plan, or around the underlying assumptions?
- Does a common language and picture exist for discussion strategy?
- Are new strategies analyzed and well planned, before implemented, or does the organization test ideas through strategic experimentation?
- Is the portfolio of the strategic experiments well balanced along the dimensions time, risk, and aim?
- How well does the innovation portfolio reflect your strategic goals?
- How well is strategy communicated and understood within the organization?
- Have the barriers to implementation been addressed?

The Process of Strategic Innovation

	Do not agree	Partially agree	Agree	Activity	Phase
Our culture makes it hard for people to put forward novel ideas.	1	2	3	In-house idea generation	High scores indicate that your company may be an **Idea-poor company.**
People in our unit come up with very few good ideas on their own.	1	2	3		
Few of our innovation projects involve team members from different units or subsidiaries.	1	2	3	Cross-pollination among businesses	
Our people typically don't collaborate on projects across units, businesses, or subsidiaries.	1	2	3		
Few good ideas for new products and businesses come from outside the company.	1	2	3	External sourcing of ideas	
Our people often exhibit a "not invented here" attitude – ideas from outside aren't considered as valuable as those invented within.	1	2	3		
We have tough rules for investment in new projects – it's often too hard to get ideas funded.	1	2	3	Selection	High scores indicate that your company may be a **conversion-poor company.**
We have a risk-averse attitude toward investing in novel ideas.	1	2	3		
New-product-development projects often don't finish on time.	1	2	3	Development	
Managers have a hard time getting traction developing new businesses.	1	2	3		
We're slow to roll out new products and businesses.	1	2	3	Diffusion	High scores indicate that your company may be a **diffusion-poor company.**
Competitors quickly copy our product introductions and often make pre-emptive launches in other countries.	1	2	3		
We don't penetrate all possible channels, customer groups, and regions with new products and services.	1	2	3		

Figure 19 - Rating your Company's Innovation Value Chain (Hansen and Birkinshaw 2007)

6. The Context of Strategic Innovation

"We shape our environments, then our environments shape us."

(Winston Churchill)

Research has shown that certain organizational factors favor not only the development of creative ideas and innovative strategies as described above, but also the successful implementation of these.

Furthermore Senge (1996) has revealed that when people are placed in the same system, however different they might be, they tend to produce similar results. Thus the argument, that by creating the according organizational environment, innovation can be promoted and encouraged (Tushman and O'Reilly III 1997).

This chapter will deal with the organizational context and the necessary elements to support the emergence, further development, and execution of strategic innovation.

The problem of whether to create such an environment and the necessary capabilities internally, through a spinout, or acquisition, and the issue of building ambidextrous organizations, capable of handling both, day to day business and innovation will thereby be neglected in favor of concentrating on the specific organizational requirements for strategic innovation. Furthermore, the industry and international contexts will also be ignored.

According to De Wit and Meyer (2004) the organizational system is defined by its:

- **Structure**, referring to the clustering of tasks and people into smaller groups;
- **Processes**, referring to the arrangements, procedures and routines used to control and coordinate the various people and units within the organization;
- **Culture**, referring to the joint understanding, shared beliefs and behavioral patterns shared by the members of the organization;
- **Members** of the organization.

Govindarajan and Trimble (2005), define the organizational DNA as being defined by its:

- **Structure**: Formal reporting structure, decision authority, information flows, task/process flows;
- **Staff**: Leadership traits, staffing policies, competencies, promotion policies, career paths;
- **Systems**: Planning, budgeting, and control systems, business performance evaluation criteria, incentive/compensation systems;
- **Culture**: Notions about behaviors that are valued, embedded business assumptions, decision biases.

Markides (2000) uses a similar definition, referring to the elements:

- **Culture**, including norms, values, and unquestioned assumptions;
- **Structure**, compromising not only the formal hierarchy but also the physical set up and its systems;
- **Incentives**, both monetary, and nonmonetary;
- **People**, including their skills and capabilities;

adding that the elements again need to fit with and support each other.

Considering these definitions, the following framework for the organizational system is suggested (Figure 20).

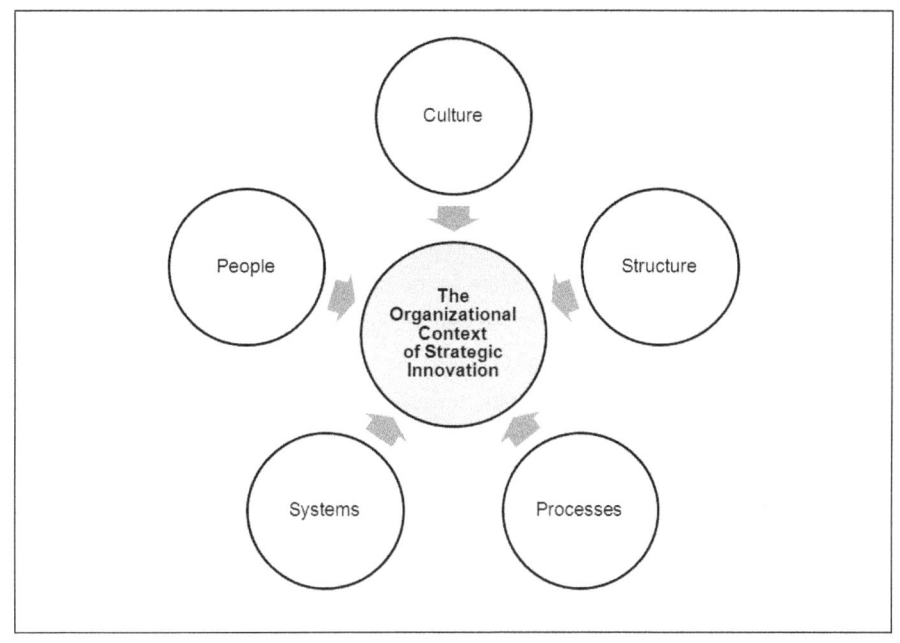

Figure 20 - The Organizational Context of Strategic Innovation

Having discussed some of these dimensions throughout this study, the following part will focus on additional issues to consider, and provide summaries of the above said, the aim being to provide an additional framework managers can consider to think about the issues involved in strategic innovation from a different point of view and to create awareness for critical success factors.

Culture

As we have seen throughout this study, challenging existing mental models and questioning established assumptions and the current status quo is a fundamental element of strategic innovation. Thus the argument that such a questioning attitude needs to be part of the corporate culture (Lynn, Morone et al. 1996; Markides 1997; Geroski 1998; Hamel 1998; Hamel 1998; Markides 1998; Kim and Mauborgne 1999; Markides 1999; Markides 1999; Markides 1999; Markides 2000; Hamel 2001; Kreuz 2001; Markides 2001).

A questioning attitude is reinforced by constantly carrying out strategic experiments as seen above, encouraging the discovery of new perspectives (Hamel 1998) and doing things differently, which can be achieved by acknowledging and rewarding success (Markides 2000), as well as failure, but punishing inaction (Sutton 2001).

It is also suggested the culture should promote teamwork and collaboration, fun and excitement (Kim and Mauborgne 1999; Markides 2000; Joyce, Nohria et al. 2003)

Joyce, Nohira et al. (2003) add that performance based cultures inspire all to do their best, reward achievement with praise, and pay-for-performance, but keep raising the performance bar. The work environment of such cultures is furthermore challenging, and satisfying.

Kim and Mauborgne (1999) add that a culture acknowledging individuals' intellectual and emotional worth and recognizing them as human beings worthy of respect regardless of hierarchical level, instead of referring to them as "labor", "personnel", or "human resources" will promote the sharing of ideas, loyalty, and voluntary collaboration for the welfare of the company.

Furthermore the culture should welcome change and be ready to accept a new strategic innovation even if it disrupts the status quo (Markides 1999).

Kreuz (2001) has shown that strategically innovative companies do not simply react to changes in the environment, but exhibit the capability to change proactively. Tushman and O'Reilly (1997) add that two main norms are needed to promote creativity: (1) support for risk taking and change, (2) and a tolerance of mistakes, both personal and organizational.

Structure

A specific organizational structure can also foster such a questioning, creative and innovative culture.

A central element to such a structure are small groups, teams and units consisting of not more than a few hundred people, or even less (Tushman 1997; Kim and Mauborgne 1999; Markides 2000; Kelley 2001), the argument being that small groups are more creative and more likely to overcome obstacles (Kelley 2001). According to Kelley (2001) great projects and products are the result of great teams.

Kim and Mauborgne (1999) argue that these small units or teams should focus on a common basis or product goal rather than organizing on the basis of function, region or channel type.

Kanter (2004) also identified a frequent contact across functions, a tradition of working in teams and sharing credit widely, as well as a structure consisting of many centers of power with at least some budgetary flexibility as being supportive to creativity.

Nonaka (1991) adds that creating new knowledge requires making insights available for testing and use by the company as a whole.

Another element of such a structure is to keep the organization fast and flat through elimination of redundant organizational layers, bureaucratic structures and behaviors, while putting the "...best people closest to the action and keeping the frontline stars in place" (Joyce, Nohria et al. 2003).

Streamlining and simplification of line-management structures and failed matrix approaches is also encouraged by Bryan and Joyce (2005). They further put forward the deployment of off-line teams to discover new wealth-creating opportunities.

Processes

Tushman and O'Reilly (1996) add that units should not only be kept small, but also autonomous (Kotter 1996; Tushman and O'Reilly III 1997) so that employees feel a sense of ownership and are responsible for their own results, which in turn encourages action. They furthermore suggest to keep decisions as close to the customer as possible.

Kim and Mauborgne (1999) argue that some degree of freedom heightens a sense of ownership among team members, promotes creativity, and ensures that individual expertise is fully exploited.

Decentralized decision making is also supported by Clemons and Santamaria (2002), and Kreuz (2001), who found employees of strategic innovators to be empowered and encouraged to act as entrepreneurs.

As we have seen above traditional strategy development processes have their limitations, and thus a new process focusing on creative exploration has been proposed.

To summarize again, it can be said that compared to the traditional planning process, the strategy making process of strategically innovative companies is characterized by being both deliberate and emergent, not relying on historical patterns, i.e. strategy does not rely on simply increasing last year's plan and budget, and the creative exploration of new options and learning through strategic experimentation (Kreuz 2001).

Furthermore, the argument for a fast, flat, and simple structure should be added to the entire processes within the organization.

Systems

Systems of course need to be adapted to the new philosophy of strategic innovation and the new strategy making process.

This means that the planning, budgeting, and control systems have to be adapted accordingly. As has already been discussed this entails primarily creating systems to capture ideas throughout the entire company, and creating new incentive and compensation systems, focusing on rewarding risk taking and experimentation, and punishing inaction. Regarding compensation, Markides (2000) notes that individual recognition might be more important than salaries, bonuses, or promotions, while Kanter (2004) adds reward systems need to emphasize investment in people and projects, and in case of strategic innovation in the abovementioned strategic experiments. Tushman and O'Reilly (1997) have found recognition from management, colleagues, and other being much more powerful than monetary rewards.

Kreuz (2001) has found the use of information technology having an influence on strategic innovation. As with the shift from operational effectiveness to differentiation, strategically innovative companies use information technology, including the internet, beyond improving efficiency, reducing costs or increasing the speed of doing business to create competitive advantage and increase barriers to entry by establishing closer and more responsive relationships with customer, beyond simply opening new, online sales channels. Examples include the use of IT to create individual customer solutions by recognizing customer preferences and buying patterns, or linking various departments by providing real time access to the entire customer data.

As we have seen above it is important to address every step in the buyer utility cycle. Information technology can certainly be used to achieve this or for reconceiving the activity system and the value chain.

Information technology can further be used to increase collaboration among employees, knowledge sharing and the exchange of information or to create knowledge marketplaces, talent marketplaces and formal networks stimulating the creation and exchange of intangibles as suggested by Bryan and Joyce (2005; 2007).

Furthermore systems that rely on performance measurements rather than supervision to get the most from self-directed professionals need to be created (Bryan and Joyce 2005; Bryan and Joyce 2007).

Clear milestones and review mechanisms have also to be established (Hamel and Prahalad 1989; Kim and Mauborgne 1997; Kim and Mauborgne 2005)

In order to ensure the necessary variety in people hiring and promotion systems also need to be adapted accordingly.

People

Besides the mentioned variety of people needed in the organization, Markides (2000), Kim and Mauborgne (1999), as well as Joyce, Nohira et al. (2003) argue that voluntary cooperation between people and the entire company is crucial to innovation.

Additionally, it seems worth repeating that strategy development is not the domain of the top management team, but of the entire organization and everybody whose support for execution is crucial. This involvement also means that ideas are treated equally, no matter whom they come from (Kreuz 2001).

Concerning people, Kreuz (2001) also found that strategically innovative companies often rely on external people to bring in new perspectives or to challenge assumptions.

Of course employees also need to be trained in the necessary skills not only to work effectively (Hamel 1998), but also, as seen above, the underlying logic of strategic innovation and change (Kotter 1996).

Table 12 summarizes the key context dimensions, which can again be used to assess the strategic innovativeness of an organization.

Dimension	Characteristics of strategically innovative companies
Culture	- Questioning attitude - Rewards success and failure, punishes inaction - Tolerates mistakes - Welcomes change - Supports risk taking and change - Supports teamwork and collaboration
Structure	- Fast and flat - Small units - Encourages collaboration - Autonomous teams at the front line
Processes	- Fast and unbureaucratic - Decentralized decision making - Support idea generation, experimentation and execution
Systems	- Support the process of strategic innovation - Enable collaboration - Enable the use and creation of knowledge - Reward risk taking and action - Used to create relationships with customers
People	- Variety (internal and external) - Collaboration - Educated in regard to the strategy and skills needed

Table 12 - The Context Dimensions of Strategic Innovation

7. The Dimensions of Strategic Innovation

To summarize part two we can say that the essence of strategic innovation is to question existing beliefs and challenge conventional logic. Strategic innovation is a new mind-set for thinking about strategy. The goal is to shift the strategic focus from beating competition to achieving competitive advantage through differentiation. Such differentiation can be achieved by creating new markets, new business models, or new value.

The content dimensions provide a framework of the issues to consider on the quest for this differentiation, while the process portrayed here is a possible way to do so. The context provides an additional dimension, the elements of which enhance and support this shift and the questioning attitude, as well as fostering creativity and innovation within the organization.

The questions accompanying every dimension will help managers to confront both, their own cognitive maps and those of their companies, spark the creative thinking process, and enable a first step towards the questioning attitude needed for innovation.

Although the three dimensions content, process, and context provide different views on the same problem, it is crucial to recognize their interdependency. To understand the whole, every dimension must be addressed. The dimensions do not represent elements that can be dismantled or addressed separately. They rather constitute a system (Figure 21).

- Culture
- Structure
- Processes
- Systems
- People

Context

The Dimensions of Strategic Innovation

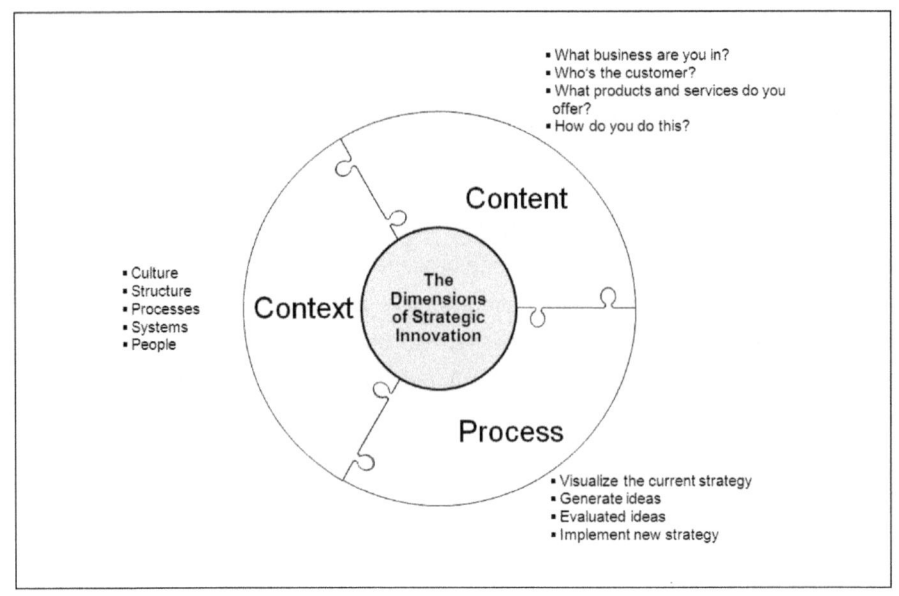

Content
- What business are you in?
- Who's the customer?
- What products and services do you offer?
- How do you do this?

Process
- Visualize the current strategy
- Generate ideas
- Evaluated ideas
- Implement new strategy

Figure 21 - The Dimensions of Strategic Innovation

Part three
The Role of Top Management

Part three will outline a set of general principles leaders should be aware of. Besides the organizational context fostering innovation, leadership plays a vital role. What that role is will be outlined in this part.

8. How to lead for Strategic Innovation

Having outlined the dimensions, issues to consider, and ingredients to strategic innovation, the question remains what managers can do specifically and what their role in leading strategic innovation is.

Bryan and Joyce believe there can be no better use of a CEO's time than to design organizations and "...develop organizational capabilities that help companies thrive no matter what conditions they meet" (Bryan and Joyce 2007). Thus top management is in charge of establishing the organizational environment (Mang 2000) featuring the traits outlined above.

Gosling and Mintzberg also argue that leaders do not do the things that organizations get done, but "...help to establish the structures, conditions, and attitudes through which things get done" (Gosling and Mintzberg 2003).

Pascale (1999), as well as Bartlett and Ghoshal (1995) agree that leaders have to set the context, within which the necessary processes can take place.

Christensen and Raynor (2003) argue a senior manager needs to be in charge of separating the ideas that have the potential for disruption, make sure that the promising ones go through the process and get the necessary resources. According to them, these tasks, and the responsibility for the process, cannot be delegated.

Markides (Mang 2000; Markides 2000) and Hamel (1998) argue along the same lines, stating that only top management can take the strategic decisions on who, what, and how, setting the parameters and boundaries within which the company and its employees are free to operate.

To make strategic innovation happen management must clearly communicate the company's commitment to strategic innovation and articulate its underlying logic (Kim and Mauborgne 1999). Management must provide clear and consistent signals about what is important and should be attended to and what is unnecessary. This way management can help employees focus and interpret events in strategically appropriate ways (Tushman and O'Reilly III 1997).

As seen such a commitment can be achieved by instilling a sense of urgency (Hamel and Prahalad 1989; Kotter 1996; Markides 2000) to illustrate the need for change. The aim is to drive out the conventional competition-based thinking, leading only to the incremental improvements (Kim and Mauborgne 1999). Top management can continuously challenge proposed strategic plans based on the dimensions and questions suggested in this study for employees to gradually shift their thinking toward the new principles.

Management is also in charge of making sure the three principles of the fair process, (1) engagement of people in decisions that affect them, (2) explaining final decisions, and (3) establishing clear expectations of actions and deliverables, as suggested by Kim and Mauborgne (1999; 2005), are respected in the strategy process.

As we have seen, a barrier to innovation is the fear of losing the valued status quo. Kim and Mauborgne (2000) argue that management has to "educate the fearful", namely employees, business partners, and the general public, to overcome the barrier of fear, by engaging in an open discussion about why strategic innovation is necessary, explaining its merits, and set clear expectations and how the company will address the issues involved.

Hamel and Prahald argue that the challenge for top management is to develop "...faith in the organization's ability to deliver on tough goals, motivating it to do so, and focusing its attention long enough to internalize new capabilities" (Hamel and Prahalad 1989), such as the capability to be strategically innovative.

Kanter (2004) identified a rather participative management style for innovation characterized by the following traits:

- Persuading more than ordering;
- Building a team, which, among other things, entails frequent staff meetings and considerable sharing of information;
- Seeking inputs from others – asking for ideas about users' needs, solicitating suggestions from subordinates, welcoming peer review;
- Acknowledging others' stake in the project;
- Sharing rewards and recognition willingly.

She adds that innovative managers are comfortable with change, have a clear sense of direction, are very thorough and persuasive (Kanter 2004). Pearson (2002) shares the argument that innovative leaders welcome change.

Gosling and Mintzberg (2003) suggest a more general management model based on collaboration, which interestingly fits the one of innovative managers, being characterized by the following qualities:

- Managers help people do the important work of developing products and services.
- Effective leaders work throughout the organization as an interacting network, not a vertical hierarchy. They do not sit on top.
- "Out of these networks emerge strategies, as engaged people solve little problems that grow into big initiatives.
- Implementation is the problem, as it cannot be separated from formulation. That is why committed insiders are necessary to come up with the key changes.
- To manage is to bring out the positive energy that exists naturally within people. Managing thus means inspiring and engaging, based on judgment that is rooted in context.
- Rewards for making the organization a better place go to everyone. Human values, many of which cannot be measured, matter.
- Leadership is sacred trust earned through the respect of others." (Gosling and Mintzberg 2003)

Amabile, Hadley et al. (2002) found time pressure to have negative impacts on creativity. "Complex cognitive processing takes time, and, without some reasonable time for that processing, creativity is almost impossible." (Amabile, Hadley et al. 2002)

Thus, the argument management should shield creative teams from time pressure and encourage them to learn, to play with ideas, and to develop something truly new.

Furthermore employees who are supposed to be doing creative work, should be shielded from interruptions and distractions (Amabile, Hadley et al. 2002). In case pressure cannot be avoided, managers should help people understand why tight time frames are necessary. Managers should also encourage one-on-one collaborations and discussions (Amabile, Hadley et al. 2002).

As been outlined earlier, rewarding people is an important element of a strategically innovative company's culture. Tushman and O'Reilly (1997) argue managers must align their rewards systems considering five key factors. Managers should think comprehensively about rewards, emphasize intrinsic rewards, ensure tight linkages between rewards and outcomes, capitalize on social learning and avoid routine.

Leonard and Strauss put forward that a "...manager successful at fostering innovation figures out how to get different approaches to grate against each another in a productive process...Such a manager understands that different people have different thinking styles: analytical or intuitive, conceptual or experiential, social or independent, logical or values driven. She deliberately designs a full spectrum of approaches and perspectives into her organization – and she understands that cognitively divers people must respect the thinking styles of others. She sets ground rules for working together to discipline the creative process. Above all, the manager who wants to encourage innovation in her organization needs to examine what she does to promote or inhibit creative abrasion" (Leonard and Straus 1997).

Summarizing the above said, top management must:

- Set the context;
- Guide the process in a participative and fair way;
- Clearly communicate reasons, and expectations and educate employees;
- Shield creative teams from distractions and pressure;
- Appreciate distinctiveness in people and their thinking;
- Welcome change;
- Ask itself what it does to promote or inhibit the innovation process and how to get rid of these obstacles.

Conclusion

"...we never gonna survive, unless we get a little crazy."

(Seal)

The purpose of this book was to:

(1) summarize and structure the current research and theories on strategic innovation,

(2) synthesize these insights and partial solutions from different authors into a comprehensive approach facilitating a systematic way for thinking through the issues involved, and

(3) provide a practical framework and advice for managers on how to think about strategic innovation, while giving a picture as complete as possible.

Having identified the need for strategic innovation by outlining some criticism and limitations of the traditional strategic management processes, tools, and theories, strategic innovation was suggested as a new mind-set for thinking about strategy. The chosen approach was to summarize the current literature using the content, process, and context dimensions as proposed by De Wit and Meyer.

Considering that every strategic problem is determined by its content, process, and context, using this problem driven approach will enable managers and researchers alike to think about the issues involved in a more comprehensive way and address the challenge from multiple angles, instead of relying on the usual step-by-step tool driven approach.

Not only has this book structured existing research using this issue based framework, but it has also drawn a more comprehensive and holistic picture of the elements to consider within each of the three dimensions, being aware though that there are certainly many more elements to consider and the particular situation of each company will probably ask for an adaptation of the elements of each dimension, tools and approaches described and suggested.

Nevertheless, while the book does not provide a final answer or even an answer to all the questions one might have, and it can be seriously doubted that there ever will be the one, it provides a more complete overview of the issues in need to be considered, instead of the usual partial solutions, and should enable organizations, managers, researchers and consultants to see the "beast as a whole" to use Mintzberg's words.

While mostly strategy literature has been considered, other sources on creativity, innovation, organizational design and change management for example have enhanced the discussion and brought in additional angles, broadening the perspective even more.

Furthermore, the strategic innovation profile suggested should encourage the search for potential for strategic innovation, as well as for measuring the level of innovativeness of a strategy and it surely represents an extension of existing tools.

Of course, there is more to strategic innovation than the scope of this study could have covered and many questions remain unanswered.

In order to build more strategically innovative and flexible organizations we need to better understand which cultural traits stimulate such a behavior, what management can and must do, and which approach yields what result under which circumstances.

As this book has shown, one conclusion seems evident: the content, process, and context of strategic innovation are fundamentally different from conventional strategy.

Strategic management is complex. Many difficult questions scream to be answered; many tough choices need to be taken. This burden should not rest on the shoulders of a selected group, i.e. senior management. Although the executive suite bears the overall responsibility, the entire company should make strategic innovation its top priority and contribute to the process wherever and whenever it can. The company as a whole should learn to think about strategy, organizational design, and how it can help everybody in the organization to perform at her best.

As we have seen there is no right or wrong answer, but as so often in life, it all depends. Every issue can be addressed from different standpoints. The key to success in strategic innovation is to be creative, to be bold, to question the status quo, by abandoning the established trail, and not be afraid to slaughter sacred cows. This holds also true for the theories, tools, and techniques offered by this study, or any study, book or article whatsoever. Companies should be more courageous, try things out, and adapt them as needed.

At the end of the day what approach a company and its management or members choose for its strategy content, process, and context, be they conventional or innovative, does not matter. The ultimate test is and will always be whether the resulting strategy enables competitive advantage and superior rents, because "unless a business has no unique advantage over its rivals, it has no reason to exist" (Henderson 1989).

References

Abell, D. F. (1980). Defining the Business: The Starting Point of Strategic Planning, Englewood Cliffs, N.J.: Prentice-Hall.

Abraham, J. L. and D. J. Knight (2001). "Strategic Innovation: leveraging creative action for more profitable growth." Strategy & Leadership **29**(1): 21-26.

Amabile, T. M., C. N. Hadley, et al. (2002). "Creativity Under the Gun." Harvard Business Review: 52-61.

Amram, M. and N. Kulatilaka (1999). Real Options. Boston, Harvard Business School Press.

Barney, J. (1991). "Firm Resources and Sustained Competitive Advantage." Journal of Management **17**(1): 99-120.

Bartlett, C. A. and S. Ghoshal (1994). "Changing the Role of Top Management: Beyond Strategy to Purpose." Harvard Business Review **72**(6): 79-88.

Bartlett, C. A. and S. Ghoshal (1995). "Changing the Role of Top Management: Beyond Structure to Processes." Harvard Business Review **73**(1): 87-96.

Beinhocker, E. D. (1999). "On the Origin of Strategy." McKinsey Quarterly **Number 4**: 167-176.

Beinhocker, E. D. (1999). "Robust Adaptive Strategies." MIT Sloan Management Review **40**(3): 95-106.

Beinhocker, E. D. and S. Kaplan (2002). "Tired of Strategic Planning." McKinsey Quarterly Special Edition: Risk and Resilience: 49-57.

Beinhocker, E. D. and S. Kaplan (2003). "The Real Value of Strategic Planning." MIT Sloan Management Review **42**(2): 71-76.

Bower, M. (2003). "Company Philosophy: The Way We Do Things Around Here." McKinsey Quarterly **Number 2**: 111-117.

Bragg, A. and M. Bragg (2005). Developing New Business Ideas: A step-by-step guide to creating new business ideas worth backing. Harlow, Pearson Education Limited.

References

Breene, T. and P. F. Nues (2005). "Understanding Competitive Essence." <u>Accenture Outlook</u> **Number 1**: 36-45.

Brown, J. S. (2002). "Research That Reinvents the Corporation." <u>Harvard Business Review</u> **80**(2): 105-114.

Bryan, L. L. and C. I. Joyce (2005). "The 21st Century Organization." <u>McKinsey Quarterly</u> **Number 3**: 25-33.

Bryan, L. L. and C. I. Joyce (2007). "Better Strategy Through Organisational Design." <u>McKinsey Quarterly</u> **Number 2**: 21-29.

Camillus, J. C. (1996). "Reinventing Strategic Planning." <u>Strategy & Leadership</u> **24**(3): 6.

Camillus, J. C. (1998). "Visionary Action: Strategy Processes in Fast-Cycle Environments." <u>Strategy & Leadership</u> **26**(1): 20-24.

Carden, S. D., L. T. Mendonca, et al. (2005). "What global executives think about growth and risk." <u>McKinsey Quarterly</u> **Number 2**: 17-25.

Chakravarthy, B. S. and R. E. White (2002). Strategy Process: Forming, Implementing and Changing Strategies. <u>Handbook of Strategy and Management</u>. A. Pettigrew, H. Thomas and R. Whittington. London, Sage Publications.

Choi, D. and L. Välikangas (2001). "Patterns of Strategy Innovation." <u>European Management Journal</u> **19**(4): 424-429.

Christensen, C. M. (1997). <u>The Innovator's Dilemma</u>, Harper Business.

Christensen, C. M. (1997). "Making Strategy: Learning by Doing." <u>Harvard Business Review</u> **75**(6): 141-156.

Christensen, C. M. (2001). "The Past and Future of Competitive Advantage." <u>MIT Sloan Management Review</u> **42**(9): 105-109.

Christensen, C. M. and J. L. Bower (1995). "Disruptive Technologies: Catching the Wave." <u>Harvard Business Review</u> **73**(1): 43-53.

Christensen, C. M., M. W. Johnson, et al. (2002). "Foundations for Growth: How to Identify and Build Disruptive New Businesses." <u>MIT Sloan Management Review</u> **43**(3): 22-31.

Christensen, C. M. and M. Overdorf (2000). "Meeting the Challenge of Disruptive Change." <u>Harvard Business Review</u> **78**(2): 67-76.

Christensen, C. M. and M. E. Raynor (2003). <u>The Innovator's Solution: Creating and Sustaining Successful Growth</u>. Boston, Harvard Business School Press.

Christensen, C. M., M. E. Raynor, et al. (2003). "Six Keys to Create New-Growth Businesses." <u>Harvard Management Update</u>.

Clemons, E. K. and J. A. Santamaria (2002). "Maneuver Warfare: Can Modern Military Strategy Lead You to Victory?" Harvard Business Review 80(4): 57-63.

Collis, D. J. and C. A. Montgomery (1995). "Competing on Resources: Strategy in the 1990s." Harvard Business Review 73(4): 118-128.

Cool, K., L. A. Costa, et al. (2002). Constructing Competitive Advantage. Handbook of Strategy and Management. A. Pettigrew, H. Thomas and R. Whittington, Sage.

Courtney, H. (2001). "Making the most of uncertainty." McKinsey Quarterly Number 4.

Coyne, K. P., R. Buaron, et al. (2000). "Gaining advantage over competitors." Retrieved July, 2005, from http://www.mckinseyquarterly.com/Strategy/Strategic_Thinking/Gaining_advantage_over_competitors_1057.

Coyne, K. P. and S. Subramaniam (1996). "Bringing discipline to strategy." McKinsey Quarterly Number 4.

Davenport, T. H., M. Leibold, et al. (2006). Strategic Management in the Innovation Economy. Publicis Wiley.

De Bono, E. (1996). Serious Creativity: Die Entwicklung neuer Ideen durch die Kraft lateralen Denkens. Stuttgart, Schäffer-Poeschel Verlag.

De Wit, B. and R. Meyer (2004). Strategy: Process, Content, Context - 3rd Edition. London, Thomson.

Demos, N., S. Chung, et al. (2001). "The New Strategy and Why It Is New." strategy+business(25): 1-5.

Drucker, P. (1993). Drucker Foundation Self-Assessment Tool. San Francisco, Jossey Bass Wiley.

Drucker, P. (1993). Managing for Results. New York, Harper Business Press.

Drucker, P. (1994). "Theory of the Business." Harvard Business Review 72(5): 95-104.

Drucker, P. F. (2002). "The Discipline of Innovation." Harvard Business Review 80(8): 95-102.

Eisenhardt, K. M. (1999). "Strategy as Strategic Decision Making." Sloan Management Review 40(3): 65-72.

Eisenhardt, K. M. and D. N. Sull (2001). "Strategy as Simple Rules." Harvard Business Review 79(1): 107-116.

Eschenbach, R. and H. Kunesch (1996). Strategische Konzepte - Management Ansätze von Ansoff bis Ulrich. Vienna, Schäffer Poeschel.

Förster, A. and P. Kreuz (2005). Different Thinking! So erschliessen Sie Marktchancen mit coolen Produktideen und überraschenden Leistungsangeboten. Frankfurt, Redline Wirtschaft.

Frazier, G. L. and R. D. Howell (1983). "Business Definition and Performance." Journal of Marketing **47**(2): 59-67.

Geroski, P. (1998). "Thinking creatively about your market: Crisps, perfume and Business Strategy?" Business Strategy Review **9**(2): 1-11.

Gluck, F., S. Kaufman, et al. (2000). "Thinking Strategically." Retrieved June, 2002, from http://www.mckinseyquarterly.com/Thinking_strategically_1068.

Godin, S. (2001). "Survival is not enough." Fast Company(54): 90.

Godin, S. (2004). "The Best Things in Life are Free." Fast Company(83): 89.

Gosling, J. and H. Mintzberg (2003). "The Five Minds of a Manager." Harvard Business Review **81**(11): 54-63.

Govindarajan, V. and A. K. Gupta (2001). "Strategic Innovation: A Conceptual Road Map." Business Horizons **44**(4): 3-12.

Govindarajan, V. and C. Trimble (2004). "Strategic Innovation and the Science of Learning." MIT Sloan Management Review **45**(2): 67-75.

Govindarajan, V. and C. Trimble (2005). "Building Breakthrough Businesses Within Established Organizations." Harvard Business Review **83**(5): 58-68.

Govindarajan, V. and C. Trimble (2005). "Organizational DNA for Strategic Innovation." California Management Review **47**(3): 47-76.

Govindarajan, V. and C. Trimble (2006). "Achieving breakthrough growth: From idea to execution." Ivey Business Journal **70**(3): 1-7.

Grant, R. M. (1991). "The Resource-Based Theory of Competitive Advantage: Implications for Strategy Formulation." California Management Review **33**(3): 114-135.

Grant, R. M. (2002). Contemporary Strategy Analysis - Fourth Edition. Oxford, Blackwell Publishing.

Hambrick, D. C. and J. W. Fredrickson (2001). "Are you sure you have a strategy?" Academy of Management Executive **15**(4): 48-59.

Hamel, G. (1996). "Strategy As Revolution." Harvard Business Review **74**(4): 69-82.

Hamel, G. (1998). "The Challenge Today: Changing the Rules of the Game." Business Strategy Review **9**(2): 19-26.

Hamel, G. (1998). "Strategy Innovation." Executive Excellence **15**(8): 7-8.

Hamel, G. (1998). "Strategy Innovation and the Quest for Value." Sloan Management Review **39**(2): 7-14.

Hamel, G. (2001). Das revolutionäre Unternehmen: Wer Regeln bricht gewinnt. München, Econ.

Hamel, G. (2002). "Innovation Now!" Fast Company(65): 115.

Hamel, G. and G. Getz (2004). "Funding Growth in an Age of Austerity." Harvard Business Review **82**(7/8): 76-84.

Hamel, G. and C. K. Prahalad (1989). "Strategic Intent." Harvard Business Review **67**(3): 63-76.

Hamel, G. and C. K. Prahalad (1990). "The Core Competence of the Corporation." Harvard Business Review **68**(3): 79-91.

Hamel, G. and C. K. Prahalad (1997). Wettlauf um die Zukunft. Vienna, Wirtschaftsverlag Carl Ueberreuter.

Hamel, G. and L. Välikangas (2003). "The Quest for Resilience." Harvard Business Review **81**(9): 52-63.

Hammer, M. (2001). The Agenda: What every business must do to dominate the decade. New York, Crown Business.

Hammonds, K. H. (2001). "Michael Porter's Big Ideas." Fast Company(44): 150.

Handy, C. (1980). "Through the Organizational Looking Glass." Harvard Business Review **58**(1): 115-121.

Hansen, M. T. and J. Birkinshaw (2007). "The Innovation Value Chain." Harvard Business Review **85**(6): 121-130.

Harari, O. (1999). Leapfrogging the Competition: Five Giant Steps to Becoming a Market Leader, Prima Publishing.

Henderson, B. D. (1989). "The Origin of Strategy." Harvard Business Review **67**(6): 139-143.

Hinterhuber, H. H. (1989). Strategische Unternehmensführung - Band 2. Berlin - New York, Walter de Gruyter.

Hinterhuber, H. H. (1996). Strategische Unternehmensführung - Band 1. Berlin - New York, Walter de Gruyter.

Hinterhuber, H. H. and W. Popp (1992). "Are You a Strategist or Just a Manager." Harvard Business Review **70**(1): 105-113.

Hippel, E. v. and R. Katz (2002). "Shifting Innovation to Users via Toolkits." Management Science **48**(7): 821–833.

Hoffmann, W., W. Klien, et al. (1996). Strategieplanung. Controlling. R. Eschenbach. Stuttgart, Schäffer-Poeschel.

Huy, Q. N. and H. Mintzberg (2003). "The Rhythm of Change." MIT Sloan Management Review **44**(4): 79-84.

Itami, H. (1987). Mobilizing Invisible Assets. Cambridge, Mass., Harvard University Press.

Joyce, W. F., N. Nohria, et al. (2003). What Really Works: The 4+2 Formula for Sustained Business Success. New York, HarperBusiness.

Judge, P. C. (2001). "How will your company adapt?" Fast Company(53): 128-139.

Kambil, A. and E. Eselius (1999). "Value Innovation in the eEconomy." A Working Paper from the Accenture Institute for Strategic Change **September 1999**.

Kanter, R. M. (2004). "The Middle Manager as Innovator." Harvard Business Review **82**(7/8): 150-161.

Kao, J. (1996). Jamming: The Art & Discipline of Business Creativity. London, HarperCollinsBusiness.

Kaplan, R. S. and D. P. Norton (1992). "The Balanced-Scorecard - Measures That Drive Performance." Harvard Business Review **70**(1): 71-85.

Kaplan, R. S. and D. P. Norton (2001). The Strategy-Focused Organization. Boston, Massachusetts, Harvard Business School Press.

Kaplan, R. S. and D. P. Norton (2004). "Measuring the Strategic Readiness of Intangible Assets." Harvard Business Review **85**(2): 52-63.

Kawasaki, G. (2000). Rules For Revolutionaries: The Capitalist Manifesto for Creating and Marketing New Products and Services, Collins.

Kelley, T. (2001). The Art of Innovation. New York, Currency.

Kelley, T. (2005). The Ten Faces of Innovation. New York, Doublebay.

Kim, W. C. and R. Mauborgne (1997). "Value Innovation: The Strategic Logic of High Growth." Harvard Business Review **75**(1): 103-112.

Kim, W. C. and R. Mauborgne (1999). "Creating New Market Space." Harvard Business Review **77**(1): 83-93.

Kim, W. C. and R. Mauborgne (1999). "Strategy, value innovation and the knowledge economy." Sloan Management Review **40**(3): 41-54.

Kim, W. C. and R. Mauborgne (2000). "Knowing a Winning Business Idea When You See One." Harvard Business Review **78**(5): 129-137.

Kim, W. C. and R. Mauborgne (2002). "Charting Your Company's Future." Harvard Business Review **80**(6): 77-83.

Kim, W. C. and R. Mauborgne (2004). "Blue Ocean Strategy." Harvard Business Review **82**(10): 76-84.

Kim, W. C. and R. Mauborgne (2005). Blue Ocean Strategy, Harvard Business School Press.

Koch, R. (2000). The Financial Times guide to Strategy: how to create and deliver a useful strategy, Prentice Hall Financial Times.

Kotter, J. P. (1996). Leading Change. Boston, Harvard Business School Press.

Kreilkamp, E. (1987). Strategisches Management und Marketing. Berlin - New York, Walter de Fruyter.

Kreuz, P. (2001). Strategic Innovation: Empirical Exploration and Development of a Conceptual Framework. International Marketing and Mangement. Vienna, Vienna University of Economics and Business Administration.

Krinsky, R. and A. C. Jenkins (1997). "When worlds collide: The uneasy fusion of strategy and innovation." Strategy & Leadership **25**(4): 36-41.

LaBarre, P. (2002). "Fresh Start 2002: Weird Ideas that Work." Fast Company(54): 68.

Leonard, D. and S. Straus (1997). "Putting Your Company's Whole Brain to Work." Harvard Business Review **75**(4): 111-121.

Leonard, D. and W. Swap (2004). "Deep Smarts." Harvard Business Review **82**(9): 88-97.

Levitt, T. (2002). "Creativity Is Not Enough." Harvard Business Review **80**(8): 137-145.

Levitt, T. (2004). "Marketing Myopia." Harvard Business Review **82**(7/8): 138-149.

Liedtka, J. (2000). "In Defense of Strategy as Design." California Management Review **42**(3): 8-30.

Linder, J. C. and S. Cantrell (2000). "Changing Business Models: Surveying the Landscape." A Working Paper from the Accenture Institute for Strategic Change.

Linder, J. C., T. H. Davenport, et al. (2003). "Toward an Innovation Sourcing Strategy." MIT Sloan Management Review **44**(4): 43-49.

Loewe, P., P. Williamson, et al. (2001). "Five Styles of Strategy Innovation and How to Use Them." European Management Journal **19**(2): 115-125.

Lynn, G. S., J. G. Morone, et al. (1996). "Marketing and discontinuous innovation: The probe and learn process." California Management Review **38**(3): 8-38.

Magretta, J. (2002). "Why Business Models Matter." Harvard Business Review **80**(5): 86-92.

Mang, P. (2000). "Strategy and Management: Constantinos Markides Discusses Strategic Innovation." European Management Journal **18**(4): 357-363.

Mankins, M. C. (2004). "Making Strategy Development Matter." Harvard Management Update **9**(5): 1-5.

Mankins, M. C. and R. Steele (2005). "Turning great strategy into great performance." Harvard Business Review **83**(7/8): 65-72.

Markides, C. (1997). "Strategic Innovation." Sloan Management Review **38**(3): 9.

Markides, C. (1998). "Strategic Innovation in Established Companies." Sloan Management Review **39**(3): 31-42.

Markides, C. (1999). "A Dynamic View of Strategy." Sloan Management Review **40**(3): 55-63.

Markides, C. (1999). "In Search of Strategy." Sloan Management Review **40**(3): 6-7.

Markides, C. (1999). "Six Principles of Breakthrough Strategy." Business Strategy Review **10**(2): 1-10.

Markides, C. (2000). All the right moves - A guide to crafting breakthrough strategy. London, Harvard Business School Press.

Markides, C. (2001). "Strategy as Balance: From "Either-Or" to "And"." Business Strategy Review **12**(3): 1-10.

Markides, C. and C. D. Charitou (2003). "Responses to Disruptive Strategic Innovation." MIT Sloan Management Review **44**(2): 55-63.

Markides, C. and C. D. Charitou (2004). "Competing with Dual Business Models: A Contingency Approach." Academy of Management Executive **18**(3): 22-36.

May, M. J., P. Anslinger, et al. (2003). Managing for Today & Tomorrow: Strategy & the High Performance Business, Accenture Report.

McCarthy, D. J. (2000). "View from the top: Henry Mintzberg on strategy and management." Academy of Management Executive **14**(3): 31-42.

McGrath, R. G. and I. C. MacMillan (1995). "DISCOVERY-DRIVEN Planning." Harvard Business Review **73**(4): 44-54.

Mintzberg, H. (1987). "Crafting Strategy." Harvard Business Review **65**(4): 66-75.

Mintzberg, H. (1987). "The Strategy Concept I: Five Ps For Strategy." California Management Review **30**(1): 11-24.

Mintzberg, H. (1987). "The Strategy Concept II: Another Look at Why Organizations Need Strategies." California Management Review 30(1): 25-32.

Mintzberg, H. (1993). "The Pitfalls of Strategic Planning." California Management Review 36(1): 32-43.

Mintzberg, H. (1994). "The Fall and Rise of Strategic Planning." Harvard Business Review 72(1): 107-114.

Mintzberg, H. and J. Lampel (1999). "Reflecting on the Strategy Process." Sloan Management Review 40(3): 21-30.

Mintzberg, H. and J. A. Waters (1985). "Of Strategies, Deliberate and Emergent." Strategic Management Journal 6(3): 257-272.

Mintzberg, H. and F. Westley (2001). "Decision-making: It's not what you think." MIT Sloan Management Review 42(3): 89-93.

Nambisan, S. and M. Sawhney (2007). "A Buyer's Guide to the Innovation Bazaar." Harvard Business Review 85(6): 109-118.

Nattermann, P. M. (1999). "Best practice doesn't equal best strategy." McKinsey Quarterly Number 4: 38-45.

Nonaka, I. (1991). "The Knowledge-Creating Company." Harvard Business Review 69(1): 96-104.

Nordström, K. A. and J. Ridderstråle (2002). Funky Business. Sweden, Pearson Education Limited.

Ogilvy, J. (2003). "What Strategists Can Learn from Sartre." Strategy + Business(33): 2-10.

Ohmae, K. (1982). "Foresight in Strategic Planning." McKinsey Quarterly.

Ohmae, K. (1982). The Mind of the Strategist: The Art of Japanese Business. New York, McGraw Hill.

Ohmae, K. (1982). "The Secret of Strategic Vision." Management Review 71(4): 8-13.

Ohmae, K. (1988). "Getting Back to Strategy." Harvard Business Review 66(6): 149-156.

Osterwalder, A. (2004). The Business Model Ontology: A Proposition in a Design Science Approach. Lausanne, Université de Lausanne: Ecole des Hautes Etudes Commerciales.

Pascale, R. T. (1999). "Surfing the Edge of Chaos." Sloan Management Review 40(3): 83-94.

Pearson, A. E. (2002). "Though-Minded Ways to Get Innovative." Harvard Business Review 80(8): 117-124.

Peters, T. (1998). Der Innovationskreis. Düsseldorf, Econ Verlag.

Peters, T. (2000). The Death Knell for "Ordinary": Pursuing Difference, tompeterscompany!

Peters, T. (2003). Re-Imagine: Business Excellence in a Disruptive Age. London, Dorling Kindersley Ltd.

Pettigrew, A., H. Thomas, et al., Eds. (2002). Handbook of Strategy and Management, SAGE Publications.

Porter, M. E. (1985). Competitive Advantage: Creating and Sustaining Superior Performance, Free Press.

Porter, M. E. (1996). "What is Strategy?" Harvard Business Review **74**(6): 61-78.

Prahalad, C. K. and V. Ramaswamy (2003). "The New Frontier of Experience Innovation." MIT Sloan Management Review **44**(4): 12-18.

Prahalad, C. K. and V. Ramaswamy (2004). "Co-creating unique value with customers." Strategy & Leadership **32**(3): 4-9.

Prahalad, C. K. and V. Ramaswamy (2004). The Future of Competition: Co-Creating Unique Value with Customers. Boston, Harvard Business School Press.

Roos, J. (2004). "Sparking Strategic Imagination." MIT Sloan Management Review **46**(1): 96.

Roussel, C. J. and P. F. Nunes (2003). "Innovation by the bundle." Accenture Outlook(3): 51-57.

Sanders, T. I. (1998). Strategic Thinking and the New Science: Planning in the Midst of Chaos Complexity and Change, Free Press.

Sawhney, M., R. C. Wolcott, et al. (2006). "The 12 Different Ways for Companies to Innovate." MIT Sloan Management Review **47**(3): 75-81.

Senge, P. (1996). Die Fünfte Disziplin. Stuttgart, Klett-Cotta.

Slywotzky, A. and R. Wise (2003). "Double-Digit Growth in No-Growth Times." Fast Company(69): 66.

Smit, S., C. M. Thompson, et al. (2005). "The do-or-die struggle for growth." McKinsey Quarterly **Number 3**.

Stalk, G. and R. Lachenauer (2004). "Hardball: Five Killer Strategies for Trouncing the Competition." Harvard Business Review **82**(4): 62-71.

Sutton, R. I. (2001). "The Weird Rules of Creativity." Harvard Business Review **79**(8): 94-103.

Thomke, S. (2001). "Enlightened Experimentation: The New Imperative for Innovation." Harvard Business Review **79**(2): 67-75.

Thomke, S. and E. Von Hippel (2002). "Customers as Innovators." Harvard Business Review **80**(4): 74-81.

Tushman, M. L. (1997). "Winning Through Innovation." Strategy & Leadership **25**(4): 14-19.

Tushman, M. L. and C. A. O'Reilly III (1996). "Ambidextrous Organizations: Managing Evolutionary and Revolutionary Change." California Management Review **38**(4): 8-30.

Tushman, M. L. and C. A. O'Reilly III (1997). Winning through Innovation. Boston, Harvard Business School Press.

Webber, A. A. (2000). "Why can't we get anything done?" Fast Company(35): 168.

Weick, K. E. (1996). "Drop Your Tools." Administrative Science Quarterly **41**(2): 301-313.

Wells, S. (1998). Choosing the Future, Butterworth-Heinemann.

Wolpert, J. D. (2002). "Breaking Out of the Innovation Box." Harvard Business Review **80**(8): 76-83.

Yates, L. and P. Skarzynski (1999). "How do Companies get to the Future?" Management Review **88**(1): 16-22.

Ziegler, R. (2002). "Anybody here have any bright ideas?" Accenture Outlook **Number 1**: 50-57.

Zook, C. (2004). Beyond the Core: expand your market without abonding your roots. Boston, Harvard Business School Press.

About the Author

Marc is a senior consultant at Doujak Corporate Development, where he leads international client engagements on issues of strategy, innovation, change, leadership and the holistic development of organizations across a wide range of industries. He is also in charge of the development of new thinking on management, innovation and strategic change and renewal.

He has worked with major corporations in Europe, the US, Canada, Latin America, Saudi Arabia, the UAE, Turkey, China and South Africa.

Besides his corporate work, Marc has also run courses at leading business schools including Stanford's Graduate School of Business, the Boston University School of Management, and the European Business School London.

Next to his consulting work, he conducts academic research focusing on processes enabling radical strategic outcomes like described in this book and what top management does to facilitate such processes.

You can find more information and read his blog at www.sniukas.com.

Visit www.reshapingstrategy.com for resources, tools and downloads supporting your journey to new markets, increased value and business model innovation.

VDM publishing house ltd.

Scientific Publishing House

offers

free of charge publication

of current academic research papers, Bachelor's Theses, Master's Theses, Dissertations or Scientific Monographs

If you have written a thesis which satisfies high content as well as formal demands, and you are interested in a remunerated publication of your work, please send an e-mail with some initial information about yourself and your work to *info@vdm-publishing-house.com*.

Our editorial office will get in touch with you shortly.

VDM Publishing House Ltd.
Meldrum Court 17.
Beau Bassin
Mauritius
www.vdm-publishing-house.com

Lightning Source UK Ltd.
Milton Keynes UK
UKHW040717220420
361997UK00003B/1092

9 783639 261103